PREVENTIVE PSYCHOLOGY
AND THE CHURCH

Books by GLENN E. WHITLOCK
Published by THE WESTMINSTER PRESS

From Call to Service: The Making of a Minister
Preventive Psychology and the Church

PREVENTIVE PSYCHOLOGY AND THE CHURCH

by Glenn E. Whitlock

w

THE WESTMINSTER PRESS
Philadelphia

PUBLISHED BY THE WESTMINSTER PRESS ®
PHILADELPHIA, PENNSYLVANIA

PRINTED IN THE UNITED STATES OF AMERICA

Library of Congress Cataloging in Publication Data

Whitlock, Glenn E.
  Preventive psychology and the church.

  Bibliography: p.
  1. Pastoral counseling. 2. Pastoral psychology.
3. Mental hygiene. I. Title.
BV4012.2.W44   253.5   72-8359
ISBN 0-664-20959-9

To
Elliott and Carole

Contents

Part III

CRISIS INTERVENTION COUNSELING
AND PREVENTIVE PSYCHIATRY

99

Foreword

Intimate acquaintance with both the developing theory and practice of preventive measures in mental health and the continuing education of clergymen has included some interesting experiences. These experiences have resulted in an awareness and an appreciation of the importance of the application of psychological knowledge to the problems of the community.

These past years have marked a developing interest in the collaboration between various professions in meeting the needs of community mental health with a *preventive* model. Although therapeutic measures will continue to be utilized to meet the needs of persons severely impaired by various levels of emotional conflicts, it makes good sense to work at a preventive level. When it is recognized that any such program demands the cooperation and collaboration of various elements of the community, the professional with primary responsibility for mental health is impelled to examine his role.

The purpose of this book is to focus attention upon the problem and promise of community mental health as it relates to the collaboration between the mental health professions and the church and temple. It discusses the commitment of both the clergyman and the mental health professional to the valuing of persons. The specific focus is upon the way the needs of the community can be met with a model of *preventive* psychiatry or psychology. The book is directed first to the

clergyman who is sensitive to the needs of specific persons and
to the needs of the community as a whole. Secondly, it is directed to the mental health professional who is open to ex-
panding his role of therapeutic activity through consultation
and collaboration with the "care-givers" in the community.

This book has been developing ever since I enrolled for
special training in crisis intervention counseling with the
Benjamin Rush Center in Los Angeles in 1965. I had been involved in providing psychological consultation and in planning conferences and workshops in the program of continuing
education for clergymen. The initial commitment in the training at the Center was related to serving as a clinical instructor
in a course offered to clergymen by the Division of Social and
Community Psychiatry, University of Southern California Department of Psychiatry.

The offering of this and subsequent courses on crisis intervention counseling was related to the concern of both the
Los Angeles County Department of Mental Health and the
Mental Health and Clergy Committee to provide consultation and training for clergymen to meet community mental
health needs.

During these years I was engaged in various dimensions of
community mental health and specifically in crisis counseling.
Having been involved concurrently in consultation for clergymen, planning for programs enhancing the development of
community mental health, and in providing direct service to
persons in crisis situations, I have had an opportunity to
reflect on the function and meaning of the program outlined
in this book.

My reflection led me to put some of my experiences in
writing. Some initial reactions have been published, and some
portions of this book have been revised from earlier papers.
Chapter 3 appeared as "Pastoral Psychology and Preventive
Psychiatry" in *Pastoral Psychology*, April, 1970. Portions of
Chapter 4 have been revised from "Psychotherapy and a Christian Understanding of Man" in *Pastoral Psychology*, February,

1967. Portions of Chapters 9 and 10 were first included in a paper presented to the American Association of Pastoral Counselors, meeting in Los Angeles in 1966, which was published in *The Pastoral Counselor*, Winter, 1967. One case study included in Chapter 11 appeared in "Emotional Crises of Those Facing the Draft" in *Pastoral Psychology*, April, 1968, and a portion of the same chapter was revised from "The Pastor's Use of Crisis Intervention" in *Pastoral Psychology*, April, 1970. Revision and elaboration on the theory and practice of crisis intervention was developed largely through extension classes taught at the University of California, Riverside, in 1970 and 1971.

In the preparation of this book, there are several persons who may be singled out for a special note of appreciation. First, there are those persons who trusted me in the midst of their crises. There are my teachers in crisis intervention, Gerald Jacobson, M.D., Wilbur Morley, Ph.D., and Martin Strickler, M.S.W., who together directed the Benjamin Rush Center. William J. Sullivan, M.D., has been both a colleague in consultation with ministers and a personal friend. Doris Stockman, colleague and friend, prepared the manuscript. My appreciation extends to my fellow faculty at Johnston College, an experimental college open to new ventures in education and to the development of our *own* psychology of a community. And finally, my gratitude to Emalee, Carole, and Elliott, who bring both sustaining and celebrative notes to my life.

G. E. W.

Johnston College
University of Redlands
Redlands, California

Part I

THE RELATIONSHIP
OF THE CHURCH
TO PREVENTIVE PSYCHIATRY

Clergymen today are involved in community mental health whether they acknowledge it or not. People search them out during personal crises, and they are often involved in some kind of relationship with those in the mental health field. The clergyman is a natural ally in preventive mental health precisely because he is involved in the daily struggles of people. He is in a position where he may intervene to prevent some crises, and where he may provide the basis for an adaptive resolution of other crises. He is available both to the members of the congregation that he serves and to the larger community within which he works.

As a member of one of the professions referred to as "caregivers," the clergyman is a natural participant in community mental health. Although his motivations may not be the same as those of people involved in preventive psychiatry, he does have an important role to fulfill. His role in primary prevention includes the traditional area of his pastoral ministry.

Part I of this book begins with the need for a concept of pastoral care and counseling that is sufficient to cope with the problem posed by community mental health. The analysis of pastoral care and counseling is made within the context of that care as practiced in the history of the church. Concepts of preventive mental health and historic pastoral care are compatible in both theological development and pastoral practice. Theology has concerned itself with a holistic view of man, and the ministry of the church has been involved in meeting persons in the normal physical, mental, and spiritual crises of their lives. In the light of both historic theory and practice and the development of contemporary community psychiatry, a model of professional cooperation and interaction has been worked out that should be helpful to the church in fulfilling this role in our modern urban world.

1

A New Approach to Pastoral Care and Counseling

In its usual expression, the model of pastoral counseling in the modern period, at least since World War II, was based on the medical model: a person comes to an office for regularly scheduled interviews. The psychological and social work professions were also dependent upon this model in their counseling and psychotherapeutic work. Although the model has served the various disciplines well in the initial development of counseling and psychotherapy in their respective fields, each of the professions has recently been developing new models for their work. Even psychiatry, which is a medical specialty itself, has had the same problem of being limited to the medical model. However, the recent development of the field of preventive psychiatry has provided a new model for at least a part of psychiatric practice. Psychologists and social workers have become increasingly involved in the area of preventive mental health and have been involved in devising revised models for their work.

In the area of pastoral care and counseling the older model has served well in developing a literature of pastoral psychology that has become increasingly important to the church. The older model of pastoral counseling will not be discarded. It will be used increasingly by pastors who are being trained as specialists in pastoral counseling. However, this model needs to be supplemented by a newer model, especially in the area of pastoral care and counseling, by the pastor who serves a particular congregation.

The older model has not served the parish pastor adequately for several reasons. Since this model usually involves extensive individual counseling, it has normally required more time than is available to the pastor of a congregation of one hundred to five hundred persons. Since he is the pastor of the entire congregation, he cannot spend his time exclusively with relatively few people. In addition, even after the pastor has concluded counseling with particular persons, he continues in a pastoral relationship with them as members of the congregation.

Moreover, the training of the pastor has often been inadequate to meet the requirements of the older model. The counselor using the older model needs an understanding of the psychodynamics of human behavior. Such training involves extensive courses in developmental and abnormal psychology, and in personality theory. Furthermore, training in counseling theory and practice involves considerable supervision as well as courses on counseling techniques. A brief introduction to the *eductive,* or *client-centered,* approach to counseling has too often misled the pastor into thinking that his function is simply to let a person talk out his problems. He has often thought, albeit erroneously, that if a person talks enough to an attentive listener, the problems will solve themselves. Of course, an attentive listener is crucial to any counseling relationship. However, if some persons are allowed to talk endlessly, they may strengthen the pattern of verbalization without meaning and provide additional defensive intellectualization against authentic insight into their behavior. A contrary result may also occur. In talking to an interested and concerned person, they may uncover defenses which they may need at that particular time and with which the pastor will not be able to cope.

The older model of pastoral counseling did not utilize the authority inherent in the role of the pastor. As the representative of a particular community of beliefs and values, the pastor has considerable authority as he fulfills his occupational and professional role. One psychiatrist remarked casually that the pastor has a lot going for him even before the interview begins, and that he would give his "eye teeth" to have such an advantage at the beginning of a psychotherapeutic relationship. Counselors and psychotherapists often have to spend hours in establishing the kind of rapport that the pastor already possesses at the outset of a counseling relationship.

If a pastor is preoccupied with the individual sessions of the medical model, it is difficult to fulfill one of the unique functions of pastoral counseling. In counseling, the pastor's function is not to do all the counseling himself through providing direct service. The function unique to his occupational role is his opportunity to train and equip a community of pastoral care. Training laymen in a congregation to perform a *supportive* and *sustaining* ministry of pastoral care is a unique function of the church in its responsibility to the larger community. In terms of the newer model, such a function may be fulfilled through the pastoral care that persons exercise for each other in the normal groups in the church. In addition, it may be fulfilled through the establishment of a special program such as a "help line" for persons in crises, and especially for those in suicidal crises.

The model of pastoral counseling, then, is being revised at a time when behavioral sciences in general are undergoing both moderate and radical changes. It seems that one of the basic aspects of this change is that the revised model involves a more active use of the self. The influence for this change comes from various directions. Within the church and its theological expression there are subtle intrapsychic influences as well as the more obvious social pressures. Pastors are becoming more knowledgeable about self-understanding and more aware of the influence of such self-awareness upon their preaching, teaching, and their conduct of worship. There is an increasingly strong emphasis upon calling persons to responsible living through preaching and teaching. Worship is increasingly understood in terms of a rehearsal of the sense of one's identity as a member of a particular community of believers. The content of the liturgy expresses the beliefs and values of a particular community, and the experience of the liturgy in common reminds a person about where he belongs and finds his identity.

Additional influence is experienced in the church by the more obvious sociotheological pressures. As the result of theological studies in relation to sociological realities such as poverty and racial inequality, the church is experiencing a renewed sense of being involved in the world. Following World War II, with improved means of communication and travel, the world has moved closer to everyone. Some persons have experienced this closeness as a threat and they have defended themselves from such threats of closeness and involvement. Whereas racial problems in the rural areas of the South have tended to be involved with the problems of upward mobility in terms of educational and political privileges, this same problem of upward mobility in urban areas tends to be concerned with housing and job opportunities. The urban housing problem is almost always involved with restrictive covenants that keep racial minorities from living too close to the Caucasian majority. In addition, urban newspapers have reported acts of beatings and stabbings while onlookers have stood by without offering help. Such onlookers reported that they did not want to get involved. All these social problems point to the increasing responsibility of the church for closeness and involvement.

This problem of closeness has been resisted by people. It is not simply a problem of race or of color, but of values. Persons within the church as well as without have resisted this closeness, but the predominant attitude of the church has been a firm commitment to involvement in the world. Theologically, this commitment is related to the Biblical concept that God loves the world. His love is not limited to the church. In fact, the Biblical record says little or nothing about God loving the church, but it does say a great deal about God loving the world. In terms of the Christian tradition, the meaning of the incarnation of Jesus Christ is that God's love is expressed to man through another man. In the traditions of both Judaism and Christianity love of God and love of neighbor go hand in hand. Love of God is demonstrated by the way a person treats his fellowman.

The increasingly active use of the self in the revised model of pastoral counseling has also been influenced by contemporary philosophy and by the research of the behavioral sciences. Contemporary existential philosophy and the developments in psychotherapy have exerted an influence upon the general practice of psychotherapy. Emphasis upon the "here and now" in the various Gestalt therapeutic measures, the "reality therapy" of William Glasser and the "integrity therapy" of O. Hobart Mowrer and the "games theory" of Eric Berne have all emphasized a more active use of self in counseling and in psychotherapy. The "logotherapy" of the existentialist psychiatrist Viktor Frankl as well as other existentialist contributions emphasizes a more active use of self. While the value of such developments in psychotherapy is primarily as a supplement to more traditional therapies rather than as a substitute for them, their influence upon pastoral counseling is considerable. In terms of the limitations of the older model for pastoral counseling, the influences on some changes in the model, including the concept of crisis intervention, have helped pastoral counseling to integrate contemporary developments in counseling and psychotherapy with some of the historic aspects of the church's pastoral care.

The theory and practice of crisis intervention is, therefore, both an expression of preventive psychiatry and an element to be integrated in the revised model of pastoral counseling. It involves a supportive and sustaining function rather than a preoccupation with analyzing the psychodynamics of personality structure. It utilizes more directly the personality resources of the individual in crisis and is akin to ego therapy. Indeed, it opposes the ego-weakening effect of a long-term dependency relationship with the therapist. Its intention is to confront the individual as a normal adult meeting normal challenges. Crisis intervention emphasizes coping directly with the current situation and is similar to the therapies directed to the "here and now." It utilizes the important insight of reality therapy that involves facing up to a reality directly even though the individual may need to face the reality in manageable doses and not all at once. It is unabashedly involved in assisting an individual to learn more facts about some concrete reality so that he may have an increasing sense of control over the situation. It is involved in listening and in accepting negative feelings, but not without intervening at points where responsibility has been shifted to another. Finally, it utilizes significant other persons in the individual's world of relationships.

Such a dimension of counseling provides a base for the church and the pastor to become involved as significant other persons in order to fulfill a supportive and sustaining ministry to persons in the throes of a crisis. The church can fill an important gap for many persons in an urban situation by providing a substitute for one's own family. The church is uniquely fitted for such a task.

2

Links Between Historic Pastoral Care and a Revised Model of Pastoral Counseling

In the history of pastoral care and pastoral counseling there have been at least four basic functions: healing, sustaining, guiding, and reconciling. The first three have been discussed by one of the pioneers of pastoral counseling, Seward Hiltner.[1] All four have been delineated in *Pastoral Care in Historical Perspective*, an authoritative analysis of the history of pastoral care.[2]

THE HISTORIC FUNCTION OF PASTORAL CARE

The *healing* function of pastoral care involves the restoration to wholeness of an individual who has somehow been deprived of it. It includes not only recuperation from a particular illness but also the achievement of a wholeness which brings with it a higher level of spiritual insight and understanding than the individual knew in the first place.

Healing is thereby seen as both *restoration* and *advance*. The methods may include the traditional methods used in traditional ways or in some contemporary development of them. It might be referred to as the demythologizing of ancient rituals, but it is usual procedure to seek contemporary understanding of traditional ideas in the areas of philosophy and religion. The traditional methods of healing include the ritual anointing with oil, or unction; the use of prayers to saints or to relics of saints; reference to certain charismatic healers and to exorcism. All these methods are related to some type of charisma or special gift exercised by a person whose gifts set him apart by ordination, or some other form of acceptance of the gift of healing. Aside from isolated instances of so-called faith healers and some emphasis within the sacramental tradition, the traditional forms of healing by prayer, laying on of hands, anointing, or exorcism have not been used widely in Western civilization, or in the Western church. Pastors involved in the healing tradition in the Western churches have tended to become a part of a hospital team as clinically trained chaplains.

The *sustaining* aspect of pastoral care consists of a supportive function. It involves helping a person to endure and transcend a circumstance over which he may have no control. Historically, this function has consisted of *preservation* of a present adjustment, a holding of the line against any other threats to the health and wholeness of the individual; *consolation* for a tragedy that has happened; a *consolidation* and regrouping, or mobilization, of available emotional resources in which the individual "gathers himself together again"; and *redemption* involving a rebuilding of life which will bring fulfillment to the person. This kind of ministry is more important than ever in a time when the actualization of human potentialities is more important than it has ever been in the history of man, precisely because there is more of a possibility of such actualization.

The *guiding* function involves helping perplexed persons to make decisions that will provide maximum utilization of their present and future potentiality. The two basic kinds of guidance include the *eductive* approach, which works to draw out the individual's own resources, and the *inductive* method, which leads the individual to adopt an a priori set of values by which to make his decision. In the history of pastoral care this function has included *advice-giving*, which has given answers to questions on the basis of a preconceived set of principles; *listening,* which involves helping the individual to use his own resources; and what has been referred to as *devil-craft,* which involves an understanding of the demonic element in life.

The *reconciling* aspect of pastoral care functions to re-establish broken relationships between man and his fellowman and between man and God. The traditional modes of the reconciling ministry are *forgiveness,* which includes confession, penance, and absolution, and *discipline,* which provides the guidelines for behavior within a particular community of believers.

CONTEMPORARY EXPRESSION OF THE TRADITIONAL FUNCTIONS

While these four functions cannot be considered entirely separate from one another, each one has a predominant or specific emphasis which allows for an examination of each function separately. Hence, even though this brief analysis may be subject to oversimplification, some broad patterns of pastoral care may be noted. Although there may be some of each of the four aspects of pastoral care in a pastor's counseling in any historical period, there seem to be some discernible periods in which particular emphases are made. This brief discussion is limited to the modern period beginning after World War I.

Aside from some emphasis within The Episcopal Church, the *healing* functions in pastoral care in the traditional sense have been outside the institutional church. New forms of the healing ministry have been worked out using the team concept, which includes the clinically trained chaplain as a part of the medical team in the teaching hospital. The Council for Clinical Training has supervised this development and the training of chaplains for such a function.

The *sustaining* function has always been an important one

in pastoral care, but pastoral counselors have tended to reject the supportive role in the contemporary approach to counseling. They have been reluctant to preserve a present adjustment because of their emphasis upon uncovering unconscious data. Parishioners have traditionally been consoled in their distresses, and this ministry will continue to be provided. However, some pastors have been fearful of an increasing dependency of parishioners upon them when a supportive role has been provided. Pastoral counselors with special training in counseling and in the psychodynamics of behavior have tended to emphasize the uncovering of unconscious data in long-term counseling rather than the preservation or consolidation of emotional resources around a present adjustment.

The *guiding* function of pastoral care has traditionally consisted of the inductive method. An a priori set of special spiritual values has formed the basis for guiding persons to correct behavior. While devil-craft may have been an aspect of pastoral care prior to the nineteenth century, advice-giving has been the predominant type of inductive guidance since that time, up to and beyond the modern period marked by World War II. Since then, there has been an increased volume of work produced by the new discipline of pastoral psychology. This approach has tended to emphasize the eductive method of guiding. This method utilizes listening as a major factor, and it has been significantly influenced by Freudian psychology and the theory of personality and methodology developed by Carl Rogers.

The *reconciling* function of pastoral care is one that has been implicit in the Judeo-Christian tradition but is not always made explicit. Pastoral care has been involved in the exercise of forgiveness primarily within a sacramental tradition of confession, penance, and absolution. Although pastors have always counseled with families in a ministry of reconciliation, the exercise of discipline has too often been based upon a legalistic definition of correct behavior rather than upon consideration of the individual. Pastoral counselors within the modern period have emphasized a nonjudgmental attitude in counseling as the result of what has been learned about the psychodynamics of human behavior. However, as the result of this emphasis, the function of reconciliation has been neglected to the point where normal guilt is not accepted as fact and hence forgiveness is no longer recognized as necessary. Discipline has tended to become characterized as punitive and restrictive of human development rather than as providing the focus necessary for the actualization of human potential.

New Directions for Pastoral Counseling

Although it is somewhat of an oversimplification, the basic model of pastoral counseling immediately prior to and following World War II has been primarily the *eductive* method of guiding. Seward Hiltner referred to the eductive approach in an early work on pastoral counseling.[3] Carroll Wise, in his book on pastoral counseling, included an important emphasis upon *insight* as the goal in counseling.[4] Both of these pioneers in the practice and teaching of pastoral counseling were influenced greatly by the depth psychology of Freud and the methodology and theory of personality of Carl Rogers and the client-centered approach. Rogers' early work exerted a significant influence on pastors and the clinical-training movement.[5] This concern and the concern of the major publications in pastoral counseling was for the *guiding* function of pastoral care. A major emphasis within this function was the eductive methodology with its preoccupation with listening and the uncovering techniques.

Such an emphasis performed a healthy function within the pastoral ministry. Since pastors had been trained for the teaching and proclamation of a particular message, their tendency was to talk rather than to listen. Theological students were trained primarily in the use of intellectual abilities, with too little emphasis upon sensitivity in relationship to people.

Theological students were trained to formulate answers, or at least to formulate the correct question, but almost always the formulation was in cognitive terms. Theologically trained pastors, then, needed to learn to listen. Having been trained to give answers to life's difficult questions, they were not trained to learn from the "living documents" just what the questions were that needed to be answered. Hence, the discipline of listening was an important contribution to the training of pastors and in the development of specialists in pastoral counseling. However, since any area of learning needs to continue to ask new questions, it is important to suggest new approaches in pastoral counseling.

During the writing of this chapter Howard Clinebell's book *Basic Types of Pastoral Counseling* came to my attention. In it he suggested a new model for pastoral counseling. He indicated that in the 1940's and 1950's "five seminal ideas played decisive roles in shaping the literature and the approach to seminary teaching of counseling: (1) the formal *structured counseling interview* as the operational model; (2) the *client-centered method* as a normative and often exclusive methodology; (3) *insight as the central goal* of counseling; (4) the concepts of *unconscious motivation;* and (5) the *childhood roots of adult behavior.*" [6]

On the basis of his evaluation that this older model is no longer sufficient to meet the needs of the contemporary practice of pastoral counseling, he suggests a new model. It emphasizes: "(1) *Using supportive* rather than uncovering *methods;* (2) *Improving relationships* (through couple, family and group methods) rather than aiming at intrapsychic changes; (3) *Maximizing and utilizing one's positive personality resources* in addition to reducing negative factors; (4) *Coping successfully with one's current situation and planning for the future* rather than exploring the past extensively; (5) *Confronting the realities of one's situation,* including the need to become more responsible, in addition to understanding feelings and attitudes; (6) *Making direct efforts to increase the constructive-*

ness and creativity of behavior as well as feelings and attitudes; (7) *Dealing directly with the crucially important vertical dimension* (the dimension of values and ultimate meanings) in relationships as well as the horizontal dimension of physical and psychological interaction." [7]

Clinebell's purpose was to suggest the introduction of various types of counseling methodologies that would reflect the emphasis of the new model. Our purpose here is to point out the various approaches included in the crisis intervention technique that reflect the various emphases in the history of pastoral care. We are not introducing something new into pastoral counseling. We are simply presenting an approach to pastoral counseling that will recall pastors to a more complete use of some of the traditional approaches in pastoral care. This purpose reflects Wayne Oates's attitude toward the uniqueness of pastoral counseling within the Protestant tradition as "a spiritual conversation that involves both *a meeting* of two persons in the context of the Christian faith and *a dialogue* between them concerning (1) 'their way of life in times past,' (2) 'the decisive turnings in the living present' and (3) the 'consideration of the outcome of their life.' " [8]

3

Pastoral Psychology
and Preventive Psychiatry

Anyone who has worked extensively with clergymen in the capacity of consultant on the problems of counseling has become aware of the unique opportunity pastors have in the area of preventive mental health. It is not altogether novel to note that some functions of the pastor have implications for reducing the incidence of mental illness. The clergyman may be involved in the community in such a way that he fulfills an integrative function, both within the particular community of believers which he represents and between various communities of interests within the larger community. In terms of mental health in general and crisis intervention in particular there are ways in which the clergyman and the religious institution come within the concern of both community and preventive psychiatry.

PREVENTIVE PSYCHIATRY

Traditionally, psychiatry has been that branch of medicine which treats and cures mental illness and emotional disorders. Psychiatry and the psychological and social work disciplines have all used the medical model with its preoccupation with the individual patient's pathology. However, there has been an increasing recognition of additional facets of mental illness.

Studies in sociology and social psychology have increased our knowledge of the human dilemma. Awareness of the increasing complexity of human life and of contemporary institutional structures has enriched the understanding of psychiatry and of the other mental health disciplines. Hence, there has been an increased awareness of the interdependence of social and individual factors in the development and persistence of emotional pathology.

The history of preventive psychiatry has been described in some detail by Gerald Caplan.[9] Some of the unique contributions to this new field are included here in order to provide a perspective for the crisis theory within the discipline of pastoral psychology and within the concern of the church.

Preventive psychiatry is not limited in its development to any complete understanding of either individual or social impediments to mental health. It bases its approach upon that of the public health field, especially in its early history. Early practitioners of public health did not always wait until they understood the etiological factors of a disease before instituting a preventive program. It has been pointed out that the historic action of John Snow in removing the handle of the Broad Street pump in order to halt the London cholera epidemic in the nineteenth century consisted of this kind of action. Snow did not know of the existence of the cholera organism in the polluted water but had simply noted that persons who drew water from this pump contracted cholera, whereas persons who drew water from another source were not affected. The early preventive program was initiated on this basis, and contemporary public health measures follow the same pattern.

Caplan contends that psychiatry can plan preventive programs before all the results of etiological research are available. These programs would use some of their admittedly less than perfect knowledge. In a summary statement he outlines the basis of a preventive mental health program. "Insofar as we direct our programs to populations rather than to individuals, we have the chance of altering the general balance of forces so that, although not all will benefit, many may have a better chance of escaping illness. Certain individuals may have so fortunate a position or privileged a background that even apart from our program they would not become ill. Other individuals may have had the dice so loaded against them by their idiosyncratic situation and experience that no amelioration of the general community picture would be sufficient to prevent their falling sick. The target of a community program of primary prevention is the large intermediate group, consisting of individuals in whom the balance of forces is not clearly loaded in one direction or another, and who would be enabled to find a healthy way of solving life's problems if the latter are somewhat reduced or if they get a little extra help." [10]

Preventive psychiatry, then, is the all-inclusive term used to cover various areas, including crisis intervention. It refers to a body of professional knowledge, both theoretical and practical, which may be utilized to plan and carry out mental health programs of a preventive nature. Caplan suggests that these programs are planned to achieve three basic purposes:[11] (1) to reduce the incidence of mental disorders of all types in a community that is concerned about primary prevention; (2) to reduce the duration of a significant number of disorders that have already occurred in the community, all of which come within the consideration of secondary prevention; (3) to reduce the residual impairment that may result from mental illness occurring in a community. This purpose may be called tertiary prevention and has some similarity of purpose to that of secondary prevention.

According to Caplan the model of preventive psychiatry is based upon the assumption that in order not to become emotionally disordered a person needs a continual source of "supplies" commensurate with his current stage of growth and development. These supplies consist basically of three types:[12] physical, psychosocial, and sociocultural. (1) Physical supplies include such things as food, shelter, sensory stimulation, opportunities for exercise, and the like, which are necessary for physical growth and development and for the maintenance of bodily health and for protection from bodily damage. (2) Psychosocial supplies include the interpersonal needs that are experienced in relation to significant other persons who become the focus of continuing emotional relationships. Resistance to emotional disorders depends on the continuity and health of these relationships. A healthy relationship is one in which a significant other person perceives, respects, and attempts to satisfy the needs of the person in relationship. (3) Sociocultural supplies include the influences upon both the development and the functioning of personality. These influences are exerted by the customs and values of the culture and social structure, particularly in relation to the primary and secondary communities to which the person belongs.

Although the model for this preventive approach originated within the practice of psychiatry, it has specific applications for pastoral counseling, and it may be applied to the church's pastoral care in a more general sense. The discipline of pastoral psychology performs a unique function even though its sense of identity is not always clearly developed. As a separate professional or occupational discipline, it exists on the boundary between psychology and theology. It performs the function of a bridge between those in the mental health disciplines and the clergy. As a ministry, it differs only in function. Ordination as a pastor, which usually precedes psychological training for pastoral counselors, is a matter of function, not of status. Since all Christians are called to ministry, the psychiatrist, psychologist, or social worker who belongs to a particular community of believers is called to a ministry within his own profession. The pastoral psychologist and the pastor as counselor differ from the others only in function.

In some sense the pastor as counselor functions in ways similar to those of any of the other occupations concerned with counseling and mental health. If we use the model of a continuous line indicating occupational functions, there is a broad middle area of counseling or psychotherapy in which common functions are shared by the psychiatrist, psychologist, social worker, and the pastor as counselor. All counsel persons with specific problems. The only limitation of the pastoral counselor is the extent of his training, supervision, and skill. However, there is an area at one end of the continuum which contains functions specific to a particular occupational group. The function of psychological testing, for example, belongs specifically to the clinical psychologist, whereas the function of hospital treatment of psychotics belongs specifically to the psychiatrist.

The special function of the pastor as counselor involves several areas. The pastoral counselor is first of all a representative of a particular community of believers. His function is related to the values and commitments of this community. He works in the church both within the context of it as a community of believers and within it as an institution in the community alongside other institutions. The church has an institutional function within the larger community, and the professional training of the pastor may equip him to fulfill particular community mental health needs.

Secondly, from his perspective within a particular community of values and commitments, the pastor as counselor functions not only as a personal counselor but also as a trainer or supervisor of a community of believers who are in turn called to provide pastoral care for one another. A pastor may help train others to provide pastoral care in situations where members of the congregation, because of their own experiences, are especially well equipped to cope with particular crises. As a trainer the pastor also works with those in the mental health field to equip them to fulfill their ministry of pastoral care. Hence, the function of the pastor as counselor is not simply to provide the direct service of counseling, but also to prepare the particular community of believers to which he belongs for their ministry. As such, his most important function may not always be in giving direct service himself, but in referring the person to a professional trained to be most helpful to the particular person in need, or in referring a person confronting a particular crisis to someone who has faced a similar crisis. A person who has been divorced and has understood his experience may be trained to offer supportive help to a person in a similar situation.

In addition to the unique function of the pastor as counselor there is the important area of direct service. Persons consult the pastor in a variety of situations. The preventive function of the pastor as counselor is based upon the 1960 report of the Joint Commission on Mental Illness and Health, which indicated that of those professional persons to whom individuals turned in times of emotional stress, about 42 percent consulted clergymen and 29 percent sought help from physicians. Only 18 percent consulted psychiatrists or psychologists and 10 percent turned to social agencies or clinics. The problem of people in need of help is so immense, the Commission reported, that one out of every four persons said that at some time or other he had felt so concerned over a problem involving such things as marriage, parenthood, or occupation that he had considered asking someone else for help. One out of seven actually had sought help for past problems. The Joint Commission included this recommendation: "Our main concern here in recommendation for a program in attacking mental illness is the various levels of service, beginning with secondary prevention—early treatment of beginning disturbances to ward off more serious illness if possible—and continuing through intensive and protractive treatment of the acutely and chronically ill." (1961)

The pastor has a unique opportunity among other professionals in the mental health field. He is the only one who ordinarily calls in the home. A pastor trained in the psychodynamics of human behavior will be sensitive to the "danger signals" and the psychological "tilts" which may be observed in individuals and families who are in varying degrees of emotional stress. Pastors who are trained to be sensitive to these nuances of behavior have indicated that their most valuable efforts are expended through such calling. Usually pastoral calling is not very effective during the day when only the women are home. However, during the evening when families are together there is an excellent opportunity to perform a preventive function in personal and family mental health.

Granger Westberg has used a model in referring to the place of the pastor in his work with persons who become ill.[13] A similar model may be used in referring to the preventive approach of the church to crisis intervention. This model is outlined as a drama in three acts.

As the first act opens, the individual who has felt able to cope with his situation is confronted with a new and hazardous situation. It is a situation in which the social forces imping- ing upon him cause his relations with others or his expecta- tions of himself to change. It may be the loss of his job. In normal circumstances it would be a hazardous situation with which he could cope. However, in this case, the circumstances of age and economic condition may be such that he loses his self-esteem and a crisis occurs. First of all, he begins to ex- perience difficulty, and then his wife and family and finally his friends notice that something is wrong.

The second act may begin with a consultation with his family doctor about his depression and lack of energy. If the situation seems to warrant it, he may be asked to go into the hospital for a checkup. The hospital checkup is the second half of Act II.

If the checkup in the hospital does not uncover some organic pathology, Act III opens with the physician referring his patient to a psychiatrist. If depression or apathy becomes severe, the individual may be hospitalized in a psychiatric hospital.

Using this model with reference to pastoral care or counsel- ing, in ordinary situations the pastor does not enter this drama until the second half of Act II as he visits the parishioner in the hospital. The chaplain specialist in a psychiatric hospital would not normally enter until the middle of Act III of this drama.

In terms of the function of the pastor, especially with reference to preventive mental health, there is a need to change the pattern of the pastor's involvement in a crisis. He needs to enter the drama of the crisis in Act I, in the preventive role. He should come in at least at the point at which friends become aware—not to replace the function of friends, but to become involved in the preventive role concurrently with, or before, the individual enters the doctor's office. In terms of the preventive role, *ministry at any point throughout Act I may be able to reverse the process of the crisis.* In Act I, the person is in the process of mobilizing his own resources—first by himself, then with the understanding and acceptance of his wife and family, and finally with the help of friends and, it is to be hoped, of his pastor.

It is during Act I that the preventive role can be exercised, often without the intervention of a mental health specialist. This preventive role can be exercised especially in the case of a crisis. The pastor may not only have the first opportunity to work with a person in a crisis, but may also have the advantage of a previously established relationship. In a crisis the individual may not move beyond Act I, especially if the crisis leads to suicide. If he is not heard in this act, he may not be heard at all. Or, if he is unable to cope with the crisis, he may not be able to function in the other acts except as the drama of the crisis is completed with psychotic withdrawal from reality. One example of the preventive role comes from the Army. When Army personnel are referred to the mental health services, the serviceman at the outset does not come into the clinic to see the psychiatrist. A technician is sent out into the field, and because the problem is solved in the field with the technician, most persons never get to the clinic. The obvious application here is that if a person is able to see his pastor in Act I, he may never need to move to Act II or Act III in the drama of a crisis. In such a situation the pastor fulfills a role in the area of preventive psychiatry or community psychology.

4

Relationship Between Theology and the Psychological Services

There are several ways of discussing the relationship between the church and the mental health disciplines involved in preventive psychiatry. There are the theoretical problems of the relationship between theology and psychology as specific disciplines. There are also practical problems of how the clergyman may actually work with the psychiatrist, clinical psychologist, or social worker, and what contribution each can make to the other. A definition of the nature of the relationship between theology and psychology, and the development of a conceptual model of a working relationship between the clergy and the mental health professionals, are necessary to any program of cooperation between the church and preventive psychiatry.

There are those who insist that there is no reason for a relationship between theology and psychology. Such persons perceive these disciplines as separate entities, with no necessary relationship between them. However, in the field of theology there are two subjects of study: God and man. In its study of man, theology needs to learn what psychology is saying about man. It is not that the behavioral sciences know all the answers, but they are discovering important things about man, and theology needs to listen to them and to remain in dialogue with them. Any competent theology has to include a competent psychology. A theology that does not learn from the behavioral sciences is answering questions that contemporary man is not asking. It is detached from what is actually happening to man and hence is irrelevant. In a similar vein, it is important for psychology and the behavioral sciences to listen to and to maintain a dialogue with theology. Some psychotherapists, for example, have attempted to eliminate any concern with values. They have suggested that it is time to "exorcise the metaphysical gremlin." However, the areas of values and religious symbolization exercise an influence that cannot be ignored by these therapists without neglecting the nature of the whole man.

THE BEHAVIORAL SCIENCES' CONTRIBUTION TO THEOLOGY

First of all, the theologian needs to listen to what the behavioral sciences are saying about man.[14] The religionist may tend to reduce everything to fit into a particular metaphysical or religious system. Such an approach is essentially a theologism, or a particular form of reductionism. In this case empirical data is rejected if it does not conform to a system of preconceived metaphysical notions. This position tends to put God in a box by limiting the area of his action to a particular system or category of thought. To the theologian, however, God is at work in the world in either physical or mental healing. If healing occurs in psychotherapy, God is active in it and the theologian needs to discover just how he is acting. The theologian's discovery of how God acts in psychotherapy comes through study of the clinical evidence of the psychotherapist.

Protestant Christian theology tends to reflect a simple moralism. A common expression about an emotionally disturbed person in the church has been, "If only he had enough faith, he wouldn't have any emotional problems." A person may be overheard saying of an alcoholic, "If only he would just use his willpower, he could stop drinking right now." Historically,

Protestantism has consistently rejected such an attitude or moralism. However, Protestant Christians have too often reflected this inadequate picture of man. The insights of psychotherapy remind the theologian that such a view of man is inadequate. Therefore, psychology and the behavioral sciences have influenced Christian theology first of all in the direction of its view of man. Any simple moralism or Pelagianism is rejected, and man is understood in terms of his estrangement, or alienation, in which he is unable to help himself—all by himself.

The research and the practice of the behavioral sciences have helped theology to take the whole man seriously. In terms of recognizing the real predicament of man in his alienation from God, from himself, and from others, psychotherapy has helped theology to discover that conscious verbalization alone is not sufficient. Man is not just a cognitive being. He embraces both a conscious and an unconscious dimension to life. Man is a symbol-making creature. He creates images and symbols, and reason alone is inadequate to cope with the whole man. Anyone who has sat quietly with a regressed schizophrenic knows that talk is not enough to meet man at his deepest level of need. The churches need to learn the truth that life consists of more than the rational. Churches that have emphasized the aspect of logic and reason in their theological approach need to rediscover the Biblical understanding that knowledge exists not only as a cerebral function, but that it is the involvement of the total person. Man arrives at his knowledge not only through rational choices, but also through experiencing the "moment of truth" in which everything else makes sense for the first time.

In addition, both contemporary psychotherapy and theology in the Judeo-Christian tradition have reminded each other that man is known only in relationship. In some periods of the history of the Christian church the Biblical understanding of man in community was ignored. According to the Hebrew view, the greatest curse that could befall a man was that he be alone. When Hosea is describing the misery of his people, he compares them to a "wild ass wandering alone." (Hosea 8:9.) Just as the normal place for the wild ass is in the herd, so the normal place for man is in the community. Certain psychotherapeutic techniques, such as group therapy and the experiments of the therapeutic communities, and recent Biblical and theological studies have attempted to help man find his way back to wholeness through a rediscovery of a sense of community.

In relation to man's understanding of man, psychotherapy has helped theology to understand that religious convictions may express sickness as well as health. Years ago in his Gifford Lectures the psychologist William James pointed out the types of healthy and unhealthy religious experiences. The behavioral sciences continue to remind theology of unhealthy types of religious experiences and expressions, and theology reminds the psychological sciences of the possible integrating nature of healthy religious experience.

A second area in which psychotherapy has influenced theology is in its understanding of God. Psychotherapy has helped Christian theology to rediscover justification by faith as a central doctrine. Even though churches retain this doctrine, it has often been interpreted in terms of a legalism against which the very doctrine protests. It has often been interpreted as another good work that a man can do all by himself. It is as if a man is able to choose his own salvation on his own grounds. Belief becomes another good work to earn salvation. Psychotherapy has helped Christian theology to regain the insight that man is not saved by his act of believing, but that man is already accepted before he believes. He is already loved, but not because he is good or deserves to be loved. He is simply loved and accepted by God. He needs only to accept the fact that God has already accepted him.

Psychotherapy has also helped Christian theology to understand that since man is a symbol-making creature, he creates symbols and images of God. Freud, in his *Totem and Taboo,* helped theology to understand that the child perceives his father as God, as the one who can do anything, the one who can do no wrong. The child does not see the real father, but makes an image of him. The father is later seen as he is, limited and not omnipotent. It is helpful for the theologian to know that man also makes images of God. This has implications for the Christian education of children, and for the communication of the knowledge of God to persons. It is important for theology to understand the implications of the psychotherapeutic problem of authority, and to understand the need of persons to work through their relationships with the mother and father who are the primary authority figures of the child. Theology needs to understand the importance of working through the problem of relationship with primary authority figures in order that the person may be free from the irrational images that he makes.

THEOLOGICAL CONTRIBUTIONS TO THE BEHAVIORAL SCIENCES

Theology has something to say to psychology and the behavioral sciences. Psychotherapy, for example, is a scientific method of treatment developed through the use of clinical evidence. However, as soon as a science moves from a pure to an applied science, a value judgment is involved. Becoming a participant in the healing process draws the therapist inescapably into the area of values. Psychotherapy is inextricably involved in values, and psychotherapists have begun to give serious consideration to this dimension of their work.[15] The psychotherapist cannot eliminate religious faith by reducing it to psychological data, as Freud attempted to do in *The Future of an Illusion*. In his conclusion Freud was simply making an epistemological decision in choosing one particular metaphysic over another. Religious faith cannot be eliminated by a metaphysical reductionism or psychologism. It cannot be explained away by psychological data. Its validity cannot be determined by the analysis of psychological data. This discussion of the validity of knowledge is the business of metaphysics, and more particularly of epistemology. Hence, psychotherapy cannot be substituted for religious faith except through a metaphysical choice.

In addition, psychotherapists need to be in lively dialogue with theologians if psychotherapy is to continue as a science. Psychotherapy learns from clinical experience. The science of psychotherapy develops through the evidence gained in psychotherapeutic practice. Whereas empirical data forms the basis of a science, it does not imply that the science is complete. Indeed, according to the scientific method, all new hypotheses must be explored if a science is to be further developed. Theology posits certain working hypotheses that are relevant for psychotherapy, and they need to be examined.

One basic hypothesis which Christian theology suggests is that a fundamental problem of man is that of ultimate authority. The Biblical account of the beginning of man is the story of creation. Man is created by God and hence is dependent upon him. In the Hebrew view of man, the flesh (*basar*) is powerless to act. It is the spirit (*ruach*) of God that enables a man to become a whole person or soul (*nephesh*). Man is created in the "image of God" with a relationship with God different from that of any of the other creatures. Man is subject, not object. He enters into an I-Thou relationship with God. Man is created a "little lower than God," and as one authority among other human authorities. The I-Thou relationship, which recognizes that man is dependent upon God and that he is created with a special relationship to God, means that man needs to work through his relationship with ultimate authority. The father and the mother fulfill particular authority roles. Just as the individual needs to work out his relationship with his parents as authority images, so he also needs to discover the meaning of existence which must be worked out in relation with the image of ultimate authority.

The Biblical account of creation is followed by the story of the temptation and the fall. Man is created with freedom to choose between good and evil. In his freedom, man transcends himself. He is free to assert himself as an end in himself, rather than as a part of the greater whole. He rejects his relationship with ultimate authority and hence sets himself both over and against his fellowmen and God. Instead of internalizing the authority that belongs to him, he attempts to exert an authority over his fellowmen that is not his to exert. Estranged man is troubled in his relationship with authority figures, both with his parents and with ultimate authority. He has rejected his relationship with God as ultimate authority, and hence he understands neither the extent nor the limitations of his own authority.

Christian theology teaches not only that God is Creator but also that he is Redeemer. He is the One who makes man whole. It is God who frees man from his estrangement and brings him back again into relationship with ultimate authority, and hence into relationship with all human authorities. Christian theologians remind the psychotherapists that while healing comes through man, it comes from a reality that transcends man. Psychotherapy itself witnesses to the fact that man cannot heal himself. Any of the self-help kits offered in popular literature are repudiated. The psychotherapist enters into relationship with the patient and healing occurs. Paul Tillich asks the questions: "How can man be the instrument for his own healing?" "Can sickness overcome itself by itself?" The answer of Christian theology is that healing power comes from beyond man, even though it comes through man. Christian theology says that God's love and acceptance, which is communicated through persons, is demonstrated or made manifest in Jesus Christ, the true man. Christian theology says that Jesus Christ is central to the problem of healing or reconciliation with ultimate authority, and hence with lesser authorities. Reconciliation is possible because in Jesus Christ man sees God in another man. Since man encounters the acceptance by ultimate authority through another man, he can begin to

accept himself. It is because man accepts acceptance by ultimate authority communicated through another man that he
can begin to internalize the authority which belongs to him,
without having to exert a distorted sense of authority over
others.

God is involved both in the process and in the outcome of
psychotherapy. It is not that Christian theology and psychotherapy are competing ideologies. It is simply that clergymen
and psychotherapists need to listen to and teach each other in
continuing dialogue. The work of the psychotherapist is to
help clear up the distortions of the emotional life so that a
person is free to choose the values to which he can be loyal.
Psychotherapy does not provide purpose in life, but it may
enable a person to choose or to respond to a life of purpose.
The work of the pastor as counselor is to help the individual
in his decision-making to choose and to respond to those values
which will give meaning and fulfillment to the whole person.

Clinical evidence from psychotherapy teaches theologians
certain things about the nature of man, so that Christian theology may be relevant to man as he experiences his deepest
needs. On the other hand, theologians need to remind psychotherapists that there are aspects of reality beyond the reach
of science. Man's coming to terms with the concept of ultimate
authority may be one of man's most basic problems. Finally,
the clergyman and the psychotherapist need to work together
directly in the area of preventive psychiatry. They need to
work together both to supplement each other's work and to
discover the ways in which metaphysical concerns contribute
either to mental illness or to mental health.

5

A Conceptual Model of the Relationship Between the Clergyman and the Mental Health Specialist

Suggestions regarding a working relationship between the clergy and the mental health professional are not new. From about 1950 to the present a number of statements have been made about both conflict and cooperation between the clergy and the mental health specialists. The presidential address to the American Psychiatric Association in 1956 was devoted to the subject.[16] The meeting of the Group for the Advancement of Psychiatry, held at the Berkeley-Carteret Hotel, Asbury Park, New Jersey, on Sunday, April 7, 1957, was reported in that group's publication as Symposium No. 5.[17]

HISTORY OF INTERDISCIPLINARY COOPERATION

Pastoral Psychology began in 1950 as a journal with an interdisciplinary approach. The first issue included articles by outstanding psychiatrists such as William C. Menninger and O. Spurgeon English, by psychologist Carl R. Rogers, and by clergymen Seward Hiltner and Russell L. Dicks. Its editorial stated: "The decision to publish our new journal grew out of an awareness of a deeply felt need on the part of the minister for the insights and skills of dynamic psychology and psychiatry presented in a way that has immediate and practical application to the minister's work, and within the religious framework of the pastor's point of view." [18] The purpose of the journal was to meet the needs of pastors serving community churches and of persons in the mental health field who had some interest in religion.

The *Journal of Pastoral Care* had been published for about four years prior to the appearance of *Pastoral Psychology*, but it represented the Clinical Pastoral Training movement and was largely limited to institutional chaplains and theological students who had received clinical training or were planning for it. This journal represented the initial movement toward clinical training for pastors which was formally organized in 1930, but which dated from the early work together of the Reverend Anton T. Boisen and Richard C. Cabot, M.D., a noted physician who also taught in the Harvard Divinity School. Dr. Cabot had introduced the case method into medical education and had a large share in the inauguration of hospital social work. From this background and as a result of his observation and work with Anton Boisen, Dr. Cabot suggested in 1925 that every student for the ministry be given a kind of clinical training for his pastoral work similar to the clinical training a medical student receives during his internship. Boisen and Cabot are recognized as the founders of the Council for Clinical Training. The formation of this Council on January 21, 1930, marked the beginning of an awareness of the need for training clergymen to work with persons in a collaborative manner with the physician. The aim of the Council was to accomplish three things: "(1) to open his eyes to the real problems of men and women and to develop in him methods of observation which will make him competent as an instigator of the forces with which religion has to do and the laws which govern these forces; (2) to train him in the art of helping people out of trouble and enabling them to find spiritual help; (3) to bring about a greater degree of mutual understanding among the professional groups which are concerned about the personal problems of men."

Underlying these aims and the whole undertaking were

three assumptions which Anton Boisen stated: "(1) that the living human documents are the primary sources for any intelligent attempt to understand human nature; (2) that the study of human ills in their terminal stages is a most important means of enabling us to grapple with them in their more complex incipient stages; (3) that service and understanding go hand in hand. Without true understanding it is impossible to render effective service in that which concerns the spiritual life, and only to those who come with a motive of service will the doors open into the sanctuaries of life." [19]

Apart from this early beginning, however, significant indications of cooperation between clergymen and mental health specialists did not appear until after World War II, and especially after about 1950. The national organization, the Academy of Religion and Mental Health, was organized in 1955 and has brought clergymen together in meaningful dialogue with mental health professionals. The Academy has organized branches in numerous cities for the continuing dialogue and for conferences on special subjects. It has issued significant publications relating to religion and mental health, and since 1961 has published the *Journal of Religion and Health*. This journal has added significantly to the growing literature on the relation between religion and the behavioral sciences, and the ways in which clergymen and mental health specialists may work together.

An additional facet of the relationship between clergy and the mental health field is the nature of the involvement of the church in contemporary social issues. Since World War II, and especially since about 1960, clergymen have become increasingly involved in social issues in a way that seems to be unique in the history of the church. The stance of involvement provides a base upon which the church may become an active participant in the area of preventive mental health. The disciplines of psychiatry and psychology have also begun to move into the area of preventive mental health along with social workers who have been traditionally involved in preventive mental health work.

As a result of the new insights about the nature of man coming from the behavioral sciences and from the change in the church's theological orientation and involvement in contemporary social issues, there is a possibility for a new kind of relationship between the clergy and the mental health disciplines. Members of the clergy have become increasingly involved in articulating the meaning of the church's witness through both the spoken word and various kinds of protest actions.[20] Interaction with those professionals who are engaged in structuring these social relationships is inevitable. As clergymen increasingly seek to translate the love of neighbor into concrete situations, the possibilities of both increased cooperation and increased tension may result from such professional interaction.

A description of the relationship between the two disciplines may be characterized by Figure 1. This figure shows the area

Function unique to the mental health profession.	Function of counseling with persons which is shared by both professions.	Function unique to the clergy.

FIGURE 1

of function which is entirely separate at some points and shared broadly at others. However, this schema does not do justice either to the complexity of the relationship or to the tensions that may exist between the professions.

A CONCEPTUAL MODEL OF A WORKING RELATIONSHIP

A more adequate conceptual framework is necessary in order to analyze the interaction processes between clergymen and mental health professionals. An analysis of the relationship between clergymen and lawyers provided the basis for the conceptual model that is developed here.[21] As practitioners, both clergymen and mental health professionals are engaged in rendering certain services to persons. Both disciplines may be involved in working with the person at different points in the process. Hence, the interaction between these professionals qua professionals will be dyadic in form. Even in a situation of consultation where a third person becomes the subject of interaction, the relationship between the parties can be conceptualized as dyads inasmuch as a triad is a series of dyads. Hence, the relationship of a clergyman to a parishioner and to the mental health professional may be characterized as three dyads as illustrated in Figure 2.

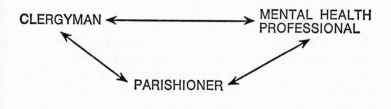

FIGURE 2

Since the clergy and the mental health professional share some mutual concerns, it is possible to differentiate modes for interaction as the members of the two disciplines work together to resolve concrete problems. As these professionals are engaged together in the process of solving a problem, they are guided by the *goals* they seek to achieve, the *values* to be preserved in the process, and the *means* that are used to achieve a solution.

Using a minus sign to indicate incongruence and a plus sign to suggest congruence, Figure 3 may be used to analyze the nature of the interaction between the clergy and the mental health profession:

GOALS	VALUES	MEANS	INTERACTION IS CHARACTERIZED BY:
+	+	+	Equal participation as autonomous professions.
−	+	+	Consultative collaboration in reference to effectiveness of treatment.
−	−	+	Collaboration on the basis of a social strategy.
−	−	−	Compartmentalized concern in which there is no professional interchange.

FIGURE 3

In Figure 3 it will be noted that as the congruence increases, there is a greater degree of interdependence as opposed to an independent self-sufficiency in professional function. At the same time, although there is an increased sense of interdependence, there is also an increase in potential interprofessional tension as the congruence of goals, values, and means increases.

By means of this analysis there are four modes of interaction that may be distinguished in the process of interaction.

1. *Equal Partners*

Interaction as equal partners in a helping discipline increases the sense of interdependence of the two professions. Each becomes a resource to the other even though each profession fulfills its function within its own context. Each of the professions shares in the helping goal, the value of health and wholeness of persons, and the means of counseling to achieve this purpose. Participation as equal partners does not mean that each does precisely the same things. They are separate professions, and each has its own function. In terms of crisis intervention, for example, each shares in the goal of helping the person to confront the reality of the crisis, of being responsible for himself in the crisis, and in the use of interventions throughout the counseling process.

2. Consultative Collaboration

This form of interaction involves collaboration by means of consultation. This consultation could be a two-way process. The clergyman could receive consultation from the mental health specialist with reference to his expertise in interpersonal dynamics. The mental health professional could seek consultation from the clergyman in terms of theological conceptualization and the meaning of religious symbols. In the area of primary prevention, mental health consultation is invaluable to the clergyman in the use of techniques such as those employed in crisis intervention. Assistance in diagnostic understanding would aid the pastor in identifying emotional problems in the incipient stages and would also fulfill a function in secondary prevention in the area of mental health. The goals of this collaboration may not be shared by the two professions, but the values to be expressed and the means to be used may be similar.

3. Social Collaboration

Interaction in terms of social strategy is crucial both in the clergyman's involvement with social issues and in the work of secondary and tertiary prevention in community psychiatry. In his concern for a comprehensive mental health program, the mental health professional will need to collaborate with the clergyman in the determination of community strategy. The establishment of comprehensive community mental health facilities is the responsibility of both the clergy and the mental health professions. Each discipline shares a concern for the mental health of persons, and the clergyman is often in a position in the community where his influence can be used in the development of a strategy to reduce the prevalence or duration of emotional disturbance and to mitigate the impairment resulting from mental illness by such means as the establishment of after-care facilities in the community. Goals and values may be dissimilar, but the means to be used would be similar.

4. Professional Compartmentalization

There may be a compartmentalization in which there is no interaction between the professions. Each functions within his own role without any interaction with the other. Goals, values, and means to be used may all be dissimilar and hence there is no interaction between them.

In addition to this description of the modes of interaction between professions, there are the ways that pastors and the mental health professions perceive their specific roles *within* their respective professions. The self-image of a professional varies according to the way he perceives his profession. In this case we are looking at the clergy and the mental health professionals only in terms of the practitioner role within their own discipline.

There have been several studies of how pastors perceive their particular professional function. Blizzard's study of the practitioner role type of clergyman is an important one.[22] According to Blizzard's analysis of empirical data, the parish minister perceives himself in terms of master, integrative, and practitioner role types. The master role is the pastor's concept of what distinguishes him from the occupational role types of other persons. The integrative role type defines the frames of reference from which the practitioner seeks to achieve his goals. The practitioner role type refers to the means and skills that are used to accomplish these goals. These various role types may be conceptualized as polarizing about the more traditional role images on the one hand, and about the more contemporary role images on the other.

The parish minister who has a more traditional self-image tends to be characterized by a master image that stresses the mediator-servant idea, an integrative role of the father-shepherd, believer-saint, or evangelist type, and a practitioner role of preacher, priest, and teacher. The parish minister with a more contemporary self-image is characterized by a master image involving functional ideas of service and example to others, an integrative role involving interpersonal involvement, and a practitioner role that involves developing a parish program, solving community problems, and an emphasis upon the ministry of pastoral care and counseling.

Although there are no studies of a similar nature on the self-image of the mental health professional, through personal experience I have noted that there are different self-images within this field. With the notable exception of the social worker, the traditional stance of the mental health specialist has been limited to the medical model of a private practice or institutional setting in which there is no necessary interaction with the clergyman. Even the social worker has tended to function as a specialist in a psychiatric setting. As the mental health professional moves away from the traditional self-image, he moves toward the development of comprehensive mental health facilities including interdisciplinary cooperation and the provision of consultative services for the other caring professions such as the clergy. Although such a characterization may be an oversimplification of the way in which persons within the mental health disciplines perceive their roles, it does seem to be a fair generalization.

The self-images of both the clergyman and the mental health specialist will influence or even determine the nature and degree of the interaction between them. The traditional image of both will emphasize professional compartmentalization and eliminate any possibility of professional interaction. To the degree that each professional moves toward a more contemporary view of his role, relevant to community needs, the degree of social and consultative collaboration increases. This collaboration may increase to the point of perceiving each other as equal partners with complete interchange and interaction on the problems of the people with whom they are jointly concerned.

INTERACTIVE RELATIONSHIPS AND TENSION

In this model of the interaction between the clergyman and the mental health professional as they move toward a more contemporary view of their roles, their interdependence upon each other increases and subsequent tensions may also increase. In the mode of interaction characterized by professional compartmentalization, there is no interaction except on a nonprofessional level. As long as two professions are kept separate they will remain alienated from each other. Both their values and the way they perceive their roles preclude any interaction as professionals. In the traditional stance of the clergyman, he will tend to reduce everything to fit into a particular theological system. In the traditional stance of the mental health professional, he will tend to eliminate the value of religious faith by reducing it to psychological data. In practice, since they see no basis for interaction, the two disciplines will simply ignore each other.

In the area of social collaboration the mental health professional may initiate the interaction and interchange because of his professional knowledge and openness to new patterns of attacking the problem of community mental health. He is more aware than ever that the problem of mental health must be met by the community as a whole and not by a single professional group. To the degree that the clergyman is aware of the need for community mental health care, he may become involved in a social strategy to provide for the necessary community programs, such as crisis clinics, day-care centers, or comprehensive mental health centers.

In the area of consultative collaboration, the clergyman who emphasizes the contemporary role of pastoral care and counseling may initiate interaction between the professions at this level of work. As he works with persons, either as individuals or in groups, the clergyman may become aware of his need to understand the dynamics of interpersonal behavior. He needs professional consultation in this area from an interpersonal specialist. To the degree that the mental health professional is aware of the significance of religious symbolization and is able to acknowledge his responsibility for values, he will need consultation and interchange with the clergyman. In this mode of interaction the clergyman has tended to be more responsive to his need for consultation from the mental health specialist, but he has also had the least to contribute to the interchange.

In the area of interaction and interchange as equal partners, there is both the greatest possibility and the greatest tension. In this mode of interaction the pastor may attempt to be an amateur psychiatrist, and the mental health professional may pretend to be an expert in theology and pastoral care. However, to the degree that each professional is aware of his need to learn from and contribute to their common dialogue, the effectiveness of the interaction will make a significant contribution to the unique functions of each. This area of interchange as equal partners holds the most promise in meeting the need for community mental health. The conceptual model outlined in this chapter may provide a basis for a systems approach to the total problem. Increasing specialization limits the approach to the total problem. Until there is a way to bring specialized knowledge and function together into a generalized frame of reference, communities will never be able to meet their needs adequately in preventive mental health.

Part II

MENTAL HEALTH
CONSULTATION
AND THE CHURCH

Consultation is a relatively new word for both the church and the pastor. Until recently there has been little or no reference to the word or to the use of this concept in the work of the church. Its usage has been common in the medical profession. It is not at all uncommon for a doctor to call in a consultant from one of the medical specialties. Indeed, as medicine, engineering, and many types of businesses have become increasingly specialized, there has been an increasing demand for consultation.

Although the church has not used the concept of consultation in the specific sense in which it is used here, it has used the ideas underlying the concept of consultation. After all, consultation is simply a request for new data upon which a decision may be made about the conduct of one's work. Pastors have always sought out such assistance from persons both within and without the institution of the church. Experienced pastors have often acted in a consultative fashion in certain occupational functions for those who were less experienced in them. Churches have sought out businessmen, administrators, and others from various occupational specialties for consultation regarding special problems that have arisen. More recently, and especially within the past ten years, the church has increasingly called consultative conferences with specialists from education, sociology, the behavioral sciences, systems analysis, and other fields. The purpose has been to learn new data about the world which confronts the church. The nature of this world is changing so rapidly that no one can know enough about contemporary developments to be able to understand what is happening without consultation with various specialists. As an expression of the renewed interest in, and commitment to the world in contemporary theology, the church is increasingly drawn to the need for various types of consultation.

Part II will examine the concept of mental health consultation as expressed through preventive psychiatry. The concepts are described in relation to a model of consultation that could be used by the church. The church's need of such consultation is discussed in conjunction with a suggested program of consultation related to the specific requirements of the churches and the pastors. Finally, various types of mental health assistance are discussed in relation to some agencies sponsoring such assistance.

6

A Model of Mental Health
Consultation
for the Church

Awareness of the need of pastors for mental health consultation is a relatively recent development. Indeed, I could find
only one reference to it in the contemporary literature of
pastoral psychology.[23] There has been considerable use of the
implicit purpose of consultation in conferences with mental
health specialists. However, it would be more appropriate to
identify such conferences as aspects of continuing education
rather than consultation as such. There are often some elements of consultation in such conferences, but their approach
is usually that of the classroom lecture with the usual period
for questions. Such conferences fulfill an important purpose,
but they can hardly be identified as consultation.

Informal consultation has taken place as pastors have sought
the counsel of mental health specialists in emergency situations. A pastor may call for assistance about what to do in
the case of a suicidal threat, the problem of hospitalization for
an emotionally disturbed person, or any such emergency problems. Although consultation in an emergency situation may be
helpful, it may be more of an attempt to get rid of a trouble-
some problem than the using of it as an opportunity for growth
and understanding.

A new development in the concept of consultation for
churches and their pastors has occurred during the past few
years. In some instances such consultation has been available

to specialized counseling services and churches. In other instances, seminars or courses have been organized under various auspices to serve the need of pastors for mental health consultation in the usual performance of their work with persons. It is this particular kind of consultation to which we now turn.

Consultation is an interpersonal contract between two professional persons, a specialist in a particular field and a consultee who seeks help in regard to a problem with which he is having some difficulty. The consultee seeks out a consultant within a field of competence in which he is having some difficulty. At the outset it must be clear that the purpose of this consultation is to assist pastors to carry out their professional responsibilities more effectively. The mental health consultant should not attempt to tell a pastor how to do his work. The consultant's function is to assist the pastor in doing what he is already doing, but in a more effective and efficient manner. The consultant is there not only to help the consultee with the immediate problem at hand, but also to give him the kind of assistance that will enable him in the future to deal more adequately with a similar type of problem.

THE NATURE OF CONSULTATION

For an understanding of the nature of consultation, it may be helpful to point out what it is not. First of all, it is not primarily *education*. Although the pastor as consultee may learn a great deal throughout the process of consultation, its primary purpose is to assist the consultee in using himself, his skill, and his training in a more effective and efficient manner. It is true that he may learn additional facts about the psychodynamics of behavior and theories of personality and counseling techniques, but this is a secondary rather than a primary goal.

Secondly, consultation is not to be confused with *psycho-*

therapy. The consultee may learn a great deal about himself in the process of consultation, but the resulting self-awareness is a secondary rather than a primary effect. The consultant does not work with the consultee in a client or patient relationship. In such a relationship there is an implicit contract in which the patient agrees to suffer the indignities of exposure in return for a promise that the professional worker will not take advantage of him in such a situation. In consultation, on the other hand, there is no such implicit or explicit contract. Although it is not the primary purpose of consultation, self-understanding will, in all likelihood, increase as a secondary result of consultation. As the pastor becomes aware of his own response to those with whom he is working, the resulting self-understanding will have a therapeutic effect upon him.

Thirdly, consultation is not to be identified with *supervision.* It is true that there are many similarities between them, but the functions differ. Whereas supervision involves two persons in the same profession, consultation does not. Supervision involves an experienced person of one profession supervising an inexperienced worker in the same profession. A consultant may be sought out from a different profession because of his expertness in that particular field. More importantly, in supervision responsibility for a client or program belongs to the supervisor, but in consultation such responsibility remains with the consultee. The consultant may clarify issues, offer diagnostic interpretations, or advise regarding treatment or counseling technique. However, the consultee may choose to accept or reject such counsel because the responsibility for the client or program remains with him.

THE TYPES OF CONSULTATION

There are four types of mental health consultation which are described in detail in Gerald Caplan's book *Principles of*

Preventive Psychiatry.[24] They will be briefly identified and discussed here, especially as they pertain to the work of the pastor and the churches.

1. *Client-centered Case Consultation*

This type of consultation, which focuses upon the client to be helped, is the one most often used by pastors. Since there is a limitation on the number of courses about psychodynamics of personality, abnormal psychology, and counseling techniques in a theological curriculum, the pastor may need professional assistance both in identifying a problem and in knowing what to do to help the individual. In psychiatric or psychological terms, this assistance may be identified as diagnosis and treatment. Knowing what underlies the behavior of a parishioner as client and determining the most effective way of dealing with him may be the kind of assistance the pastor is seeking.

In defining what constitutes client-centered consultation, Caplan points out that "the problems encountered by the consultee in a professional case are the focus of interest; the immediate goal is to help the consultee find the most effective treatment for his client. Educating the consultee so that he may in the future be better able to deal unaided with this client or class of clients is a subsidiary goal. Since the primary goal is to improve the client, the consultant's fundamental responsibility is to make a specialized assessment of the client's condition and to recommend an effective disposition or method of treatment to be undertaken by the consultee. The consultant's attention is centered on the client, whom he will probably examine with whatever methods of investigation his specialized judgment indicates are necessary in order to arrive at an adequate appraisal of his difficulty." [25]

Hence, the focus of this consultation is upon the individual parishioner. The primary purpose will be to help him, but to do this through the pastor who has already established the therapeutic relationship. Such a consultation provides for an economical use of the time of both the pastor and the mental health specialist. Since the pastor has previously established the relationship as a part of his professional role, he already has the kind of rapport which the mental health specialist would have to spend hours developing. In addition, the pastor may see an individual in the midst of a crisis situation, therefore this approach to pastoral care and counseling provides a more effective way in which the pastor and the parishioner may be helped to deal with this problem. The consideration of the theory and practice of crisis intervention will come in Chapters 9 and 10, and that elaboration will verify the importance of pastoral care and counseling with adequate consultation.

In such consultation there is a problem of communication. Of course, this problem is not unique to the professions of clergy and mental health specialist. In any area of specialization there is the inevitable development of both a vocabulary and a frame of reference unique to that profession. Hence, it is important that the consultant and the pastor as consultee understand each other. The nature of the dialogue between the two professional disciplines has been described in Chapter 4. Interdisciplinary professional associations such as the Academy of Religion and Mental Health have assisted in making each discipline more intelligible to the other. The mental health consultant to a pastor needs to understand something about theological language and thought and the pastoral frame of reference. In a previous book I have included some thoughts on the orientation of a minister.[26] In addition, there are numerous books that would give such an understanding. Some of these books are listed in the Topical Bibliography in this book, but reference may be made to two books that may be especially helpful at a relatively brief reading.[27] If the consultant understands the pastor and his work, he will be better able to diagnose the parishioner's problem and to suggest treatment which the pastor may use in his particular professional context.

The mental health consultant will also need to listen to

precisely what is being requested. The pastor may need to clarify or to have help in clarifying just what question he is asking. In describing a parishioner as client to the consultant, the pastor may be asking for assistance in working with this person or he may really be saying that he wants to refer him to the specialist. The pastor may be unsure of himself in this new territory or he may not want to work with this particular parishioner as client. The reason for not wanting to work with this person may result from the objective problem of the parishioner's being within the congregation or from subjective inner conflicts which the parishioner's problem arouses within the pastor. At any rate, the problem needs to be clarified and an acquaintance with the frame of reference within which the pastor works will help the consultant to carry out his responsibilities more effectively.

2. Program-centered Administrative Consultation

The focus of this type of consultation is upon a program and upon the administration of a program. The consultant concerns himself with the problems of the institution rather than with those of a particular person. From the psychiatric perspective Caplan writes: "In this consultation, the mental health specialist is asked for help in those problems of administration which may influence the mental health or personal effectiveness of personnel or of recipients of the program. His specialized knowledge of personality dynamics and personal relationships in social systems is exploited in order to help administrators behave more effectively and, at the same time, with a greater regard for the human needs of their colleagues, subordinates, and clients." [28]

This type of consultation may be used by the pastor and the churches in at least three different ways. First of all, problems of administering an institution involve interrelationships between the members of the professional staff and may involve their wives. Since churches are increasingly calling multiple staffs to administer the church's program, there are problems in this area. Second, there are the problems of program administration by members of the church. Since laymen are involved actively in church administration either as officers of the congregation or as leaders of content programs, the problem of personal relations between them and the professional staff is an important one. Finally, there are the problems related to the effectiveness of the content of the program itself. The mental health specialist may help a congregation to plan the kind of teaching situations that will enhance their effectiveness in the development of the church as a therapeutic community. Programs may be planned that will be preventive in nature and hence have a therapeutic influence upon the mental health of the members of the congregation. Whether or not some programs will fulfill this preventive function in relation to emotional health depends upon some factors which will be discussed in Chapter 7.

3. Consultee-centered Case Consultation

This particular type of consultation may be the most important one for the pastor and, at the same time, the least understood. Again, Caplan's description is a helpful one. "The focus of the consultant in this type of consultation is on the consultee, rather than on the particular client with whom the consultee is currently having difficulties. True, the problems of this client were the direct stimulus for the consultation request and will form the main content area of the consultation discussion, and a successful consultation will usually lead to an improvement in the consultee's handling of the current case, with consequent benefit for the client. But, in contrast to client-centered case consultation, in which the consultant's main interest is diagnosing the difficulties of the client, his primary endeavor in the present instance is to assess the nature of the consultee's work difficulty and to help him overcome it." [29]

This type of consultation is especially important to the pastor because of the predominant orientation of his theological preparation. Although there are some notable exceptions, theological schools for the most part have tended to provide a series of fragmented courses with a preoccupation on the cognitive development of their ministerial candidates. The emphasis of theological education has been to provide graduate courses in religion rather than to prepare men and women for a ministry with persons. Preparation to understand the origin and nurture of religious faith as it is correlated with contemporary developments in the world is indeed important, but it is only part of the preparation a minister needs in order to provide pastoral care for persons. In a previous book I discussed the need for self-understanding on the part of the ministerial candidate, and a continuing self-definition throughout his ministry.[30] The notion of a pastor's use of self in his pastoral work is a relatively recent concept even though it has always been accepted implicitly as a psychological requirement for the professional ministry. At any rate, clinical training has been deficient in the theological school curricula. There is still too little concern about meeting the psychological need of the pastor to understand himself in relation to those with whom he works.

There are several types of difficulties that may interfere with the pastor's ability to work helpfully with a parishioner as client. Caplan has described them as lack of professional objectivity, lack of understanding of the psychological factors involved, lack of skill or resources to deal with the problem, and a lack of confidence and self-esteem.[31] These difficulties will account for the distortions and omissions in a consultee's report on a parishioner as client. The mental health specialist will need to be able to identify the internal inconsistencies and the verbal and nonverbal cues that the pastor gives as he discusses the client. These difficulties are discussed here in relation to the ways they may be experienced by pastors.

a. Lack of professional objectivity

The implications in the use of consultee-centered case consultation are related to the use of the self of the pastor in his work of pastoral care and counseling. The pastor needs to understand himself with some objectivity in order to be open to his own feelings and emotions. As an example, he needs to understand his own sexual needs so he will not need to seek out feminine comfort in his counseling role. He needs to be sufficiently free from the projection of his own insecurities or aggressive needs onto the other person. To the degree that he is emotionally unsure of his own psychological needs, he will tend to exploit others for his own unmet needs rather than help them.

It is in this sense that the consultee-centered case consultation may be especially important to the pastor. It will continue to be a crucial need until pastors are provided with adequate supervised clinical training in their theological education. Even when adequate supervised work has been completed it will be recognized that there are times when the pastor encounters a problem with which he will need some mental health consultation. If a pastor understands his own feelings objectively in relation to the people with whom he works, he will be better equipped to help them constructively with their problems. On the other hand, if he does not understand his own feelings, he will tend to be inept at best, and possibly even destructive in his interpersonal relationships. All his efforts, of course, may be with the best of intentions, but the result will be both destructive and self-defeating.

The loss of objectivity occurs in his professional work when the pastor's own unmet emotional needs enter into the relationship with the parishioner as client. Caplan has called this difficulty a "theme interference." It is usually of an unconscious nature and is brought into focus by the problem of the parishioner as client. The subjective involvement of the pastor as counselor results in a change from *empathy* with the parishioner to *identification* with him. There is a fine line between empathetic understanding of a person's problem and identification with him, but the differentiation is important. Empathy enables a pastor to establish rapport and to assist in the resolution of the parishioner's problem. An identification with the parishioner as client confuses the counseling relationship. Identification involves a loss of objectivity, and such personal involvement leads to "a distortion of perception and judgment and a lowered effectiveness in utilizing professional knowledge and skills." [32] The pastor will be vulnerable if as a result of his personality difficulty he is currently experiencing some situational conflict in his home or in his work.

Since the theme interference is an unconscious phenomenon, there are very specific behavioral expressions which may indicate such a difficulty. These actions may serve as psychological "tilts" which could lead the pastor to such consultation. These tilts are indicators that subconscious factors are affecting the pastor's relationship to the parishioner as client.

In his pastoral care or counseling with a particular parishioner or group within the church the pastor should be sensitive to the following patterns of his own behavior:[33] (1) he develops a sudden increase or decrease of interest in a particular person; (2) he begins to feel that he simply *must* succeed with an individual or group; (3) he becomes aware that he looks for acceptance, appreciation, or praise from a particular person; (4) he is aware that he consistently becomes upset by expressions of reproach or dissatisfaction from an individual; (5) he experiences the urge to engage in professional gossip with his colleagues concerning the parishioner; (6) he begins to look forward to seeing a particular person; (7) he is threatened by the possibility of losing the closeness of a particular relationship; (8) he discovers that he consistently tends to argue or be sarcastic or unnecessarily sharp with a particular individual or group; (9) he feels compulsive about "hammering away" at certain points; (10) he becomes especially involved in doing things for a parishioner; (11) he tries to impress a parishioner or a colleague with the importance of one of his parishioners; (12) he becomes careless with appointments, forgetting, consistently being late, etc.;

(13) he consistently experiences depressed or uneasy feelings when he thinks of a parishioner; (14) he begins to dream or to have fantasies about the individual; (15) he overprotects the individual from his reality situation; (16) he provokes the individual to an excessive reaction to someone in his own environment; (17) he tries to satisfy the individual by giving advice or undue reassurance.

Although these tilts do not constitute a complete listing, they are suggestive of the kinds of guidelines that may be helpful in directing a pastor to a mental health consultant. In the eventuality that the pastor loses his sense of objectivity in his pastoral care and counseling, he will need the mental health consultant to describe to him the nature of the theme interference in a way that it will be understood and eliminated as an interference. The pastor will then be enabled to utilize his professional knowledge and skills effectively. If he does not understand what has happened in the situation, he will be unsuccessful in his professional efforts, and he will continue to project his own unmet needs upon persons in similar situations in the future.

Caplan's approach to this problem of a loss of objectivity is to separate the consultee's personal life from his work difficulty.[34] Hence, the consultant does not work with the *causes* of the theme interference, but only with defining it in relation to the context in which it occurred. Dealing with the causes of the interference draws a consultant away from his primary function and directs him toward the goal of psychotherapeutic insight. Since the pastor is using the parishioner to work out his own problem vicariously, he will be defensive about dealing with the causes of the theme interference. However, if the consultant works with the pastor in describing *how* his emotional involvement interferes with his ability to see the parishioner objectively, the pastor's perception may be improved and corrected to enable him to see the parishioner more objectively and hence, to see the situation as more hopeful for resolution.

As an example of theme interference, a pastor brought up a problem that he encountered with a man in the congregation. The man was about forty-five years of age, married, and had two children in their teens who were active in the youth group at the church. He was a salesman by occupation and served on the official board of the church. The pastor described him as a friendly, outgoing person with very conservative theological and political ideas. He was aggressive in his relationships and in his leadership roles, and was very critical of the pastor's leadership. The pastor indicated that he had repeatedly tried to talk to the man about his approach, but that he always seemed to end up in an argument, and he always felt depressed about never being able to communicate with him. When this parishioner criticized a sermon or some aspect of the church program, the pastor felt anxious and depressed even though others had expressed their appreciation. Following the presentation of the problem, the consultant directed questions to the pastor. How did he feel personally about this man? What was the nature of the man's position on the official board? Did he have the power to threaten the pastor's position?

First of all, the pastor needs to become aware of what he really feels about this person apart from what he feels he *ought* to feel. If he can become aware of and acknowledge his *real* feelings, he will be ready to explore the meaning of this person to him. He needs to become aware of his hostility toward this man and of his own frustrated aggressive needs. The consultant will not need to explore the causes of these feelings which are probably related to the pastor's difficulty with authority persons or possibly with a sibling rivalry. The consultant will focus upon an understanding of the feeling that the pastor experiences here and now in relation to this particular man. Next, the consultant needs to understand the context of the pastor's work situation. First, this man is a member of the congregation and is involved in a relationship with fellow believers in which he may need pastoral care or counseling. Secondly, he is a member of the official board of the church and hence has some power over the position and working conditions of the pastor. In other words, this man poses some objective threat. For all these reasons, the pastor cannot simply dismiss him as a nuisance or as someone with whom he will have nothing to do. Work with him is already included in the pastor's job description. However, this does not mean that the pastor has to put up with all kinds of nonsense from this man. After all, the pastor is only a man and he must attempt to do only that which may be achieved. He is not expected to be more than he is. He does not know all the answers either for himself or for others, and he is not able to do emotionally more than he can do. The needs of the pastor that motivate him to provide care for persons in the pastoral ministry are often the very needs which involve him in attempting to undertake more than he is able to do. Nevertheless, the pastor has this man with whom he must work, and he will need to differentiate between the objective threat and his subjective involvement with the man because of his own personality problem with persons in authority.

b. Lack of psychodynamic understanding

Another type of difficulty in the consultee-centered consultation is a lack of understanding of the situation, especially in terms of the psychodynamics involved. It was indicated earlier in this chapter that the usual three years of graduate theological education cannot provide the minister with an understanding of psychodynamics or psychopathology sufficient to understand the factors involved in some intrapsychic or interpersonal problems. The consultant will need to help the pastor by adding to his knowledge in these specialized areas, and to assist him in understanding how this data relates to the individual and environment in which it is expressed.

Such consultation should not be confused with teaching courses in the various areas of human behavior, especially if the consultation is on an individual basis. If the consultation is conducted with a group, such teaching may be included, but even then it would simply be a subsidiary goal.

In a situation where pastors and laymen were conducting a summer day-camp program for youngsters, two members of the staff described their problem with a particular girl. She was ten years old, and they felt she came from a difficult situation at home. Very little was known of the home, however, because the family did not belong to the church and her parents were not known to the staff. She presented problems including stealing, lying, and disrupting the group. The staff was attempting to teach the values of this particular church through the interpersonal relationships that were established at the day camp. Hence, the two teachers tried to be understanding and accepting in order to communicate these values. As a result of the type of problem which the girl presented, they protected her by relaxing the limits set for the group as a whole and by not being firm with her, thinking that she would be helped by such permissiveness. However, the girl did not respond, and the group of girls as a whole began to resent the selective use of limits. After some questioning in which it seemed clear that she did not learn from experience and that none of the staff had experienced any degree of affect, or feeling, in relation to her, the consultant pointed out that in all likelihood she was deficient in some ability to respond to feeling. In psychological terms, she did not seem to have developed an adequate superego, or conscience, with which to interact. Hence, he indicated that they might have more success with her by treating her kindly but firmly and by reminding her firmly of the reality of the group limits. Permissiveness and overprotection of such a girl would only make it more difficult for her to respond and tend to undermine the group as a whole.

c. Lack of professional skill

Although some pastors may understand the psychodynamics of a problem, they may lack the specialized skill necessary to accomplish the goal. The mental health consultant assists the pastor, first of all, to choose a particular course of action. It may be one in which the pastor is helped to understand how he can make professional use of the self more effective, or it may involve a knowledge of the appropriate community resources to which a person could be referred. Caplan points out that this type of consultation is similar to professional supervision, but it is regrettably true that pastors tend to be deficient in this type of professional training. Some such consultation might be accomplished through group instruction. One of the most helpful aspects of a recent conference on pastoral work was a section conducted by a social worker on community resources for the pastor. The Protestant Community Services of the Los Angeles Council of Churches compiled a brochure for pastors on community resources that fulfilled an important need in southern California.

Another direction of mental health assistance is the possibility of a specialized plan of therapy for a particular parishioner as client. In a situation of crisis, for example, there are specialized ways in which intervention may be planned to meet a particular need. Part III of this book will deal with the theory and practice of crisis intervention, especially as it may be used by the clergyman. The problem of bereavement is a type of crisis with which the pastor has the greatest acquaintance. Techniques to cope with it are developed in Part III.

d. Lack of confidence and self-esteem

This type of problem is probably less relevant to pastors, except for young and inexperienced ones. In such a situation the pastor would probably feel frustrated, frightened, or impotent to deal with the problem posed by the parishioner. The function of the consultant may be simply one of encouragement and ego support. A young, inexperienced pastor may feel more able to deal with a problem simply by having talked it over with a specialist.

The first time a pastor becomes aware of some suicidal threat by a parishioner, he may become so frightened that he will be immobilized by it. Of course, he may be assisted to discover the most skillful way of working with the parishioner, but the most important assistance that the consultant can give may simply be a supportive one. Such support may enable the pastor to do what he is uniquely able to do in such a situation.

4. Consultee-centered Administrative Consultation

This category of consultation involves the pastor in his administrative relationship to the church as an institution. The focus is upon the pastor as consultee, and it is similar to consultee-centered case consultation. However, it involves the pastor as he is involved in his administrative function. For this reason, the mental health consultant to a pastor needs to have some acquaintance with the kind of administrative problems that occur in the church. Of course, the nature of such problems will vary according to the polity and program of a particular branch of the church. In brief, these types are essentially the congregational form of government in which the local congregation has the final word, the episcopal system in which authority is vested in the bishop and a hierarchy of authority, and the representative or presbyterian polity in which some power is vested within the local congregation, but the final authority lies in a series of judicatories composed of elected representatives from both clergy and laymen. This brief survey of the types of government may be helpful in that it shows the varied contexts in which a pastor may be working within the Protestant tradition.

It has often been repeated that the pastor wears many hats, and that administration is one of them. In addition to everything else that he does, he administers an institution. His administrative function is to organize the institution in such a way that its *purpose* may be accomplished most effectively.

However, the primary function of church administration is not to run an institution efficiently, but to enable it to fulfill its *purpose* most effectively. Furthermore, the church is not organized simply around the pastor. It consists of laymen and clergy alike in administrative and program responsibilities. However, the pastor is the chief administrative officer and certain crucial administrative decisions are, in the last analysis, his responsibility.

Hence, administration involves not only the aspects of an institution but the total work of the pastor. Administration involves the pastor first of all in relation to the church staff consisting of additional clergymen, educational directors, ministers of counseling, secretaries, custodians, and others. Administration also involves the coordination of all the programs undertaken by the church. Although the purpose of the former type of administration may involve completing a job effectively and efficiently, the function of the church as a community of pastoral care must be maintained in the process. Part of the purpose of planning and administering a church program is to conduct it effectively, but at the same time to achieve the purpose of the church. Hence, the primary purpose of administering a church program is not efficiency, but the training of a community of persons who will fulfill the purpose of the church which involves them in society as change agents.

Since the mental health consultant's expertise is in the area of psychodynamic understanding rather than in a thorough knowledge of administrative problems, he will be more helpful in assisting the pastor in the areas of interpersonal behavior. In fulfillment of this responsibility, the mental health specialist may use either individual or group consultation. Group dynamics skills may be communicated to the consultee in a group approach to consultation, but it would be a subsidiary goal. As Caplan points out, the problem in group consultation is to handle the problem of theme interference.[35] When pastors in a group begin to expose their emotional involvement with a parishioner the group may evolve into group therapy, in which case there is no separation between personal and work problems. When the theme interference is dealt with in an experience of clinical training in a group, there are elements of both supervision and the side effects of psychotherapy.

7

The Church's Use of
Mental Health Consultation

The church's use of mental health consultation is dependent
both upon its awareness of the need for such assistance and
upon its understanding of the ways in which such consultation
will provide that assistance.

The Church's Need for Mental Health Consultation

The shocking statistics in the report of the Joint Commission
on Mental Illness and Health, referred to in Chapter 3, indicated that in terms of emotional stress, 42 percent of the people
seeking help consulted clergymen. You may recall, for contrast, that only 18 percent of these people initially consulted
psychiatrists or clinical psychologists and 10 percent consulted
social workers. The number of persons seeking out clergymen
at a time of emotional stress is revealing. As will be discussed
in Chapter 9, the only question that remains is, What happens
to these people at the time of this consultation?

About a year after the Joint Commission report, a research
study was published dealing with how leaders of various
sections of the community evaluate abnormal behavior. The
leaders selected came from four types of community activity
—political-legal, economic, educational, and religious. Catholic, Jewish, and Protestant clergymen constituted the leader-

ship of the religious community. The beginning hypothesis of the researchers was that since the educational and religious leaders were concerned with personal welfare and development in social and moral terms, they would possess a frame of reference more compatible with that of the psychiatric community than that of the other two types of leaders. The leaders evaluated fictitious case histories, using three types of evaluation: (1) judging the cases mentally ill, (2) regarding the disorders as serious, and (3) recommending help from the mental health professions. The results were surprising to the researchers and a cause for alarm to clergymen. Of the four types of community leaders, clergymen showed the lowest tendency to see mental illness in the cases presented. They seemed to have relatively high tendencies to regard the cases as serious, but it was only 57 percent over against 84 percent for educators. Most surprising of all was that clergymen showed a low tendency to advocate help from the mental health professions. Only 43 percent advocated such help compared to 88 percent for the educators, and 70 percent by the political-legal leaders. The researchers declared: "Most startling are the results on orientation of the religious leaders. These leaders tend to regard the disorders as serious, to be sure; but they showed low tendencies to judge the cases as mentally ill, and low tendencies to recommend help from the mental health professions." [36]

These results were noted despite the fact that the frequency with which they were asked for advice about problems of mental disorder was greatest. Hence, the high frequency with which they were consulted was consistent with the results of the Joint Commission report. The authors noted also: "When asked about the number of hospital patients they had known —a question that does not depend on their own definitions of mental disorder—71% of the religious leaders said they knew four or more as compared to 48% of the educational leaders." [37] Hence, although the religious leaders tended to be called upon most often for advice about problems of mental disorder because of their particular leadership positions, their orientation was the most likely to be incongruent with the psychiatric frame of reference. These results are cause for alarm, both within the clergy and the mental health disciplines.

A Program of Mental Health Consultation

The use of mental health consultation is one of the constructive actions that the church could take in response to the two researches that have just been reported. The development of such a program would not be an additional burden on the pastor, but ideally would free him to work more effectively and use his time more efficiently.

In any consideration of a program of mental health consultation for the pastor and the churches, there is the need for understanding on the part of both disciplines. The need for dialogue implies that there are two persons talking to each other from their own particular perspectives. The nature of the dialogue has been outlined in Chapter 5, but the need for interaction comes up also in relation to consultation. Pastors will need to understand that consultation for the church is a new approach. Indeed, the concept of a community approach to mental health through the various helping occupations is a relatively new concept. There is much to learn about it and patient perseverance will be needed by both disciplines. The consultant will need to understand more about the value structure and frame of reference of the pastor so he will more readily understand the personal meaning related to the pastor's grasp of his work. The pastor will need to appreciate the clinical orientation of the mental health specialist. In this plea, then, for a program of mental health consultation there is no implication that the pastor needs consultation in *all* his pastoral care and counseling. As someone once remarked, "Help is needed only when you can't walk without support, not when you're already walking satisfactorily." A pastor's readiness for such consultation is related to the objective occupational requirements of the ministry, his role concept of the ministry, his theological preparation, and his theological perspective, which includes his attitude toward the clinical orientation of the mental health specialists.

1. *Occupational Requirements of the Ministry*

Since some specific occupational requirements of the ministry have been outlined in my earlier book, it is sufficient to say here that, as an occupation, the ministry tends to have a generalist rather than a specialist function.[38] It fulfills an integrative or generalist function in the community. H. Richard Niebuhr introduces the term, "pastoral director" to delineate this conception of the ministry.[39] This concept conceives of the pastor both as a counselor and as a resource for referral. His pastoral function is either to provide the necessary care or counseling himself, or to direct the parishioner with a particular need to the specialist who can fulfill this need. The minister's pastoral function is integrative in nature, and his purpose is to discover where the need exists in the community and to be prepared to use the resources of the community to meet the need. This function may be fulfilled more effectively and efficiently with mental health consultation.

2. *Role Concepts of the Ministry*

In Blizzard's study of the ways in which ministers perceived their own function, there were fourteen different integrative roles.[40] These roles included exemplary example, evangelist, general practitioner, scholar, liturgist, father-shepherd, interpersonal specialist, parish promoter, community problem solver, educator, subcultural specialist, lay minister, representative to the church-at-large, and church politician. Only one sixth of the clergymen saw themselves fulfilling an interpersonal function. This statistic may reflect pastors' feelings of inadequacy in the interpersonal role. In more than one instance, psychiatrists or psychologists have indicated that they were surprised that pastors did not see their role as involved with interpersonal concerns. Mental health consultation would assist pastors in improving their self-image in terms of their interpersonal function and would be able to outline ways in which such a function may be helpful in the fulfillment of the pastoral role.

3. Theological Preparation

These comments about the theological education of pastors are limited to the Protestant communions. Protestant theological education, for the most part, has been predominantly concerned with theological learning. It has emphasized the cognitive development of ministerial students and minimized their emotional development. It seems that Roman Catholic and Jewish theological education is in a similar predicament. However, the theological schools are increasingly including some elements of clinical pastoral education. There are varying stages of clinical pastoral education and its purpose was defined by the 1953 National Conference on Clinical Pastoral Training as "an opportunity for a theological student or pastor to learn pastoral care through interpersonal relations at an appropriate center such as a hospital, correctional institution, or other clinical situations, where an integrated program of theory and practice is individually supervised by a qualified chaplain supervisor, with the collaboration of an inter-professional staff." [41] The theological schools still vary in the degree of emphasis they place on clinical education. Mental health consultation is no panacea for this need to develop a clinical orientation, but it can provide pastors with additional understanding of their interpersonal function in pastoral work.

4. Theological Perspectives

The theological perspective of a particular pastor and church will also influence the degree to which he will respond to mental health consultation. For this reason, the statistics reported above on the low tendency of clergymen to advocate help from the mental health profession, we should examine the differences between pastors with different theological perspectives in order to be most helpful. Although there is no exhaustive treatment of the problem of theological perspectives here, it may be helpful to look at one segment of Protestantism in terms of its attitude toward the use of any development in the behavioral sciences. Pastors and mental health specialists may be referred to a little book *Handbook of Christian Theology* for additional information, but the definition of this segment of Protestantism may be helpful in identifying the problem: "Fundamentalism is now a religious attitude rather than a religious movement. It is a highly ideological attitude. It is intransigent and inflexible; it expects conformity; it fears academic liberty. . . . It has cut itself off from the general stream of culture, philosophy and ecclesiastical tradition." [42] Such an attitude is not limited to any particular denomination and may be expressed in varying ways through nearly any of the communions. It emphasizes the attitude of the closed mind. Milton Rokeach indicated that from his studies he discovered that persons measured as dogmatic or closed in terms of a beliefs system demonstrate more difficulty than open persons in synthesizing or integrating new ideas into their world view.[43] Hence, there are pastors and churches with a theological frame of reference that resist any new development and may be especially threatened by the behavioral sciences which are involved in the study of the nature of man. Practitioners in the mental health professions who would like to read further about the differences between various theological perspectives are referred to *What Present-Day Theologians Are Thinking,*

a brief but excellent description of some contemporary theologians.[44] It is still a helpful survey even though it does not
include some of the most recent developments in theology.

THE CLINICAL ORIENTATION

An additional basis for the initiation of mental health consultation is a readiness to adopt a clinical orientation. Despite
the varying types of theological perspectives, unless his theological education has included clinical pastoral education,
the pastor is usually unequipped to really understand the
clinical frame of reference in a way that will enable him to
use it. A contemporary pastor who has graduated from a
graduate theological school is usually trained to approach his
professional work in a predominantly rational way. His equip-
ment in theological learning is important and basic to his
understanding of his purpose and function, but it is only a
part of his preparation for work with persons. Emphasis upon
the rational approach increases fragmentation and there is a
need to be aware of a symbolism by which unity can be
achieved. Even though religious concepts are rich in symbolism,
there has been a notable lack of awareness that there is a
symbolic dimension to man as a human being. The clinical
frame of reference is sensitive to symbolic meanings communicated by persons. Hence, the mental health clinician listens for
symbolic meanings. He hears the content of what is said, but
he listens for its meaning. He hears the actual words that are
spoken, but he also attempts to understand what the person
means. Words are symbols in themselves, and the counselor or
psychotherapist attempts to understand the meaning of the
symbolism at a specific time and place. In all likelihood, a
pastor's orientation will emphasize a concern for the rational
at the expense of the symbolic in interpersonal relations.

In still another way, a clinically oriented worker questions
anything that is said. Statements are not always taken at face

value, since everything that is said is not an "objective" analysis; it is always an interpretation. One's own needs and defenses provide "psychological filters" that influence one's perception and involve relative degrees of distortion. In other words, a person usually sees what he "wants" or "needs" to see rather than what is objectively there. At the same time a pastor's frame of reference tends to take statements at face value. He may be disconcerted by what he hears, but he tends to assume that the person actually meant what the *words* communicated.

The clinician is also oriented to discover the meaning of an experience to a particular person at a specific time and place. The clinical orientation reflects the philosophic influence of both pragmatism and relativism. The pragmatist is attempting to learn just what works. The relativist is preoccupied with the concrete situation. He is not interested in generalized rules of behavior that may be applied in any situation. He has seen the truth that all laws cannot be applied without ambiguity to both generalized and specific situations. In this way, the clinical orientation has influenced decision-making in every area of life precisely because it sees *persons* rather than rules. Of course, this frame of reference is not entirely new. The classic reply of Jesus to the criticism that he was breaking the commandment requiring rest on the Sabbath was that "the Sabbath was made for man, not man for the Sabbath." It may be helpful both to the mental health specialist and to the clergyman to be reminded that the Judeo-Christian tradition values persons over rules. However, institutional expressions of concern tend to be legalistic. Hence a pastor's concern for an individual may be expressed in a legalistic form of prescribing rules. Although such prescriptions are defensive maneuvers of insecure persons, pastors do represent institutions or communities of believers. With the exception of some of the sect churches, the religious traditions of Christianity and Judaism have a sense of history. They stand within the central stream of historic religious thought, and they are aware of their responsibility to preserve the wholeness of truth worked out through centuries of thought. There is a sense of historic truth that is more dependable than an exploration of a hypothesis which is, of necessity, fragmented rather than whole. However, the church continually steers between the Scylla of the responsibility to communicate its wholeness of truth to one generation after another and the Charybdis of using principles and rules to preserve such wholeness. Although such use of rules and principles contradicts the priority of persons over rules, pastors may tend to use them rather than take the risk involved in the freedom of the clinical frame of reference.

The clinical orientation also requires serious *listening*. A colleague and friend enunciated this frame of reference very clearly as he reported on his experience with his fellow pastors in a group dynamics laboratory.

"One of the hardest things for me to do is to allow the person or group to strive to seek the right answer when I know the answer. It is ego-satisfying to be the answer man. Too often, in our dealings with groups and individuals, we try to guide them into our ideas or into our specific words that we want to hear instead of allowing them to grow. We allow them to be democratic all right, but democratic to develop the point that we, as leaders, want. But even this democratic group atmosphere may become a demonic disguise under cover of which the minister unwittingly succumbs to the temptation of authoritarianism. For example, if I feel the primary purpose of my ministry is to make up the deficiencies of the religious knowledge of the layman, I will feel anxiety heightened when I am asked a question I cannot answer. If my primary purpose is to allow people to grow, including myself, then my anxiety is lessened because the purpose is for the both of us to seek the answer to this question. Very few of us are willing to admit that we dominate others, but I found in this laboratory experience that very few are aware when they are dominating and when they are crushing others into objects or things. To be an authority dispensing crumbs of religious knowledge to the multitudes is a role most of us enjoy playing. But it is not always the best learning process. Our primary function is to help others to discover the answer for themselves so that it is a real part of their experience." [45]

Hence, such orientation is not unique to the sciences. Although pastors have tended to be trained with a more rational approach, the clinical frame of reference is, in actuality, an approach that enhances the pastoral function of the clergyman. Listening provides an opportunity for both a catharsis and a supportive feeling that someone else is interested. Such listening also provides the possibility of thinking a problem through in a new way because it involves the person in search for an answer. It means that the pastor and the parishioner can struggle together to come to the right question and to some resolution of the problem. This outline of the clinical orientation is not exhaustive, but it does give some contrast between the usual approach of the pastor and that of the mental health specialist. Additional aspects of the clinical approach have been discussed in the previous chapter.

8

Programs of Mental Health
Assistance
for the Church

There are several decisions that the church and the pastor must make about the choice of a particular approach to mental health assistance. First, there is the choice of the type of consultation that would be of most help in a particular situation. These types and the ways in which they may be helpful to the church have been described in Chapter 6. The church and the pastors will need to evaluate each type of consultation in the light of how it can best serve the purpose and function of the church in the particular situation in which it is involved.

Secondly, the church will need to work out with the mental health specialist the kind of assistance that will be most helpful in various kinds of situations. There are various types of assistance that may be provided by the mental health specialists.

TYPES OF MENTAL HEALTH ASSISTANCE FOR THE CHURCH

1. *Conferences on the Pastoral Ministry*

There are one-day conferences and institutes which cover a variety of subjects. Such conferences have either had a specific theme, such as "The Suicidal Individual," or a variety of subjects around a general theme, such as "Cooperation Between

Psychiatry and Religion." The number of pastors coming to such a meeting is usually large, and the purpose is to expose these pastors to some aspect of a mental health problem in the hope that it will encourage the pastor with minimal interest to learn something about the problem and to study it further.

2. *Mental Health Seminars*

A second type of instruction is provided for pastors who wish additional preparation in the general area of mental health. It may take the form of a series of seminars, workshops, or classes. Workshops in areas such as premarital counseling and marital breakup have been conducted. A ten-week course on "Crisis Intervention Techniques for Clergymen" has helped to equip pastors for crisis counseling. University extension courses in the areas of cooperation between medicine and religion have assisted pastors to work meaningfully with medical doctors on their common concerns for mental health. This type of educational assistance usually provides course instruction consisting of lectures by specialists and discussion periods. One series of mental health seminars included the following areas: (*a*) basic concepts of emotional disorders, including definitions, normal psychologic development and its complications, and discussion and clarification of developmental psychology; (*b*) troubled persons with symptomatic complaints including the depressed person and the anxious person; (*c*) chronic personality problems that cause interpersonal difficulties, such as those involving the dependent person, the inadequate person, the compulsive person, and the psychopathic personality; (*d*) sexual problems including adolescent sexual problems, and the sexual problems of the unmarried young adult; (*e*) sexual maladjustment in marriage; (*f*) psychotic or bizarre behavior including religious fanaticism, paranoid behavior, severe depression, and marked social withdrawal; (*g*) alcoholism and drug addiction.

3. Mental Health Center Staffs

Some community mental health centers sponsor meetings with staff members. They may consist of single conferences or a series of seminars, but a basic contribution to pastors is the availability of a staff for such assistance. The Suicide Prevention Center in Los Angeles has made its services available to pastors. Some community mental health centers have opened their staff meetings to clergymen. Such an experience offers educational assistance to pastors in the handling of difficult counseling problems.

4. Group Consultation

The usual form of consultation for pastors is group consultation. A pattern that has been used successfully consists of an invitation to pastors in a geographical area to meet at regularly scheduled times with a mental health specialist. Some such consultative groups require a fee for the program, whereas others have been offered by some government or private resource as a service to community mental health. Pastors bring their counseling and administrative problems to the group meetings. The consultant asks for certain data and directs the pastor's attention to particular psychodynamic aspects of the problem. One suggested outline for pastoral case presentation asks the pastor to do the following: (a) identify the person in relation to sex, age, race, occupation, marital status, family, etc.; (b) give the chief complaint, that is, the obvious problem with which the person comes to the counselor; (c) present an overall picture of the past history of emotional problems relevant to psychiatric problems, including hospitalization, psychotherapy, etc.; (d) outline the education, position in the family, early years, personal characteristics, military history, etc.; (e) list the sociological functions including employment, where the person lives and with whom, his relationship with people, trouble with the law, etc.; (*f*) tell what the person is like in a descriptive sense such as the nature of his contact with reality, how he relates to his environment, whether his intelligence is commensurate with his education, how he relates to you, whether or not you like him, etc.; (*g*) state what seems to be going on emotionally inside this person; (*h*) state the specific problems upon which you wish to focus attention.[46]

Using such an outline of a case presentation will save the time of both the consultant and the consultee. This outline could also form the basis for case presentation and individual consultation.

Another type of group consultation is designed for the leadership of the local church. It is especially relevant for multiple staff churches that have pastors in specialized work in addition to the senior pastor and other professional personnel. In such churches there are the administrative and interpersonal problems of the professional staff itself as well as the problems encountered in the work of pastoral care and counseling with members of the community.

5. *Individual Consultation*

One aspect of group consultation consists of pastors bringing their individual problems of pastoral care and counseling to the consultant. In actuality, it is simply individual consultation in a group. The main difference between individual and group consultation is that pastors may learn from each other's failures and successes in a group situation. Group discussion of pastoral problems may be a helpful educational tool. However, one difficulty with group consultation is that pastors are often reluctant to discuss their pastoral problems with their colleagues, especially if it involves a failure. All professionals find it difficult to examine their failures, even though it is obvious that persons learn from their failures as well as from their successes.

A pattern that has been suggested by mental health specialists but which is rarely used is the monthly individual consultation in a pastor's office with additional consultation by phone or special appointment. Some pastors might need assistance on a broader scale than this, but such a pattern would provide both for more personal and more available mental health assistance. Such consultation might be provided by community agencies or it might consist of time purchased by the churches. The cost of consultative services could be a regular budget item of any church in the fulfillment of its pastoral responsibility to its membership and to the community it serves.

AGENCIES SPONSORING MENTAL HEALTH ASSISTANCE

Various types of agencies have sponsored mental health assistance to pastors and churches. The nature of this assistance may vary with the sponsoring organization, but the following list gives some indication of the varied types of community agencies that may help the church to fulfill its responsibility in preventive psychiatry by providing various resources for the pastor and the church.

1. Community citizens groups, including the local mental health association and specialized committees such as that of the Mental Health and the Clergy Committee, which is a special committee of a mental health association. These groups usually consist of an interdisciplinary and interfaith membership.

2. Government agencies, including county and state departments of mental health and the National Institute of Mental Health which has sponsored pilot projects in community mental health.

3. Community agencies, including specialized groups such as suicide prevention centers and crisis-oriented walk-in psychiatric clinics such as the Benjamin Rush Center for Problems of Living in Los Angeles.

4. Interdisciplinary groups, such as the Academy of Religion and Mental Health, which are national organizations consisting primarily of practitioners in the mental health disciplines such as psychiatry, psychology, and social work, and clergymen. Nationally, the Academy publishes a newsletter and the *Journal of Religion and Health,* which carries articles of an interdisciplinary nature. Its purpose is to increase the dialogue between the clergymen and the professionals in the behavioral sciences. Local chapters of the Academy sponsor individual meetings, seminars, and workshops according to the local needs expressed.

5. Professional associations, including county and state associations of psychiatry, psychology, and social work. In addition, the American Medical Association has a special committee on religion and medicine which is active in providing various kinds of dialogue and continuing education for the ways in which pastors and medical doctors can work together. The American Association of Pastoral Counselors is a professional association of specialists in pastoral counseling. This association provides a bridge discipline between the clergy and the mental health disciplines.

6. Local and national councils of churches provide avenues through which various types of mental health assistance may be administered. Whereas the Roman Catholic and Jewish communities have a fairly well centralized structure through which to reach the clergymen in those communions, the councils of churches or ministerial associations provide the most unified approach to the various Protestant communions. Within the councils of churches there may be departments that are staffed with professional personnel to provide direct services, committees on pastoral services that may sponsor continuing education including pastoral care and counseling, and urban training centers to equip pastors and laymen to cope with urban problems.

7. Denominational offices continue to be an important key to reaching clergymen. They are equipped to provide ready

access to personnel, and they usually possess a structure through which programs of continuing education or consulta tion may be administered. Such offices may include committees and/or professional staff with particular responsibility for clergymen in that denomination. Such a committee and/or staff may be the most effective structure through which work with clergymen may be administered if the council of churches in that area is not adequately organized or staffed.

8. Theological schools have become not only centers of theological learning for preordination training, but also for continuing education of pastors and other professional church personnel. Their curricula may include both academic and clinical training. Clinical pastoral education may involve a relationship with an institution such as a hospital or with a professional clinical-training group which has training programs in institutional settings.

9. The Council for Clinical Training has conducted clinical training programs for clergymen in various types of institutions since the 1930's. General and mental hospitals and correctional institutions with chaplains have provided the institutional settings for this training. Their purpose has been not only to train a corps of chaplains, but also to provide a minimal training for pastors of churches in community settings. The clinical training movement has been aware of the potential contribution of the parish pastor in the preventive role. Such a role functions both in relation to institutional patients who have been returned to their communities, and to the prevention of serious emotional disorders by early recognition of the signs of mental illness, and by preventive pastoral counseling.

10. Church counseling centers are a relatively new development and take different forms in different churches. They range from a pastoral counseling program that is related to a staff minister of counseling, to a service with personnel employed to provide various types of specialized services.

11. University extension courses and growth-center offerings

add another dimension to the broad area of affective or experiential education available for pastors, priests, and rabbis. Both specialized programs and consultative services can be offered through the university. The increasing involvement of the university in the issues affecting the community provides an additional resource to the clergyman and the church in the interest of both preventive planning and methods of treatment. In addition, the increased interest in cross-disciplinary studies in the colleges and universities has increased the potential for interprofessional cooperation which makes both training and preventive programs possible.

12. Individual local churches and pastors. In the final analysis the programs sponsored through local churches may be the most effective in particular situations. However, the increasing trend is to make cooperative efforts in meeting broad social problems, such as that posed by the urban crisis, including the need for preventive mental health.

THE CHURCH'S USE OF CONSULTATION IN VARIOUS STAGES OF PREVENTION

The church and the pastors will need to use consultation differently in the various stages of preventive mental health. Such consultation is related both to the way in which the pastor may understand and use his interpersonal skills, and to the way in which the community of the church may be used as a social resource.

1. *Primary Prevention*

In the first place, consultation in the stage of primary prevention is related to the use of the church as a social resource. It involves both program-centered and consultee-centered administrative consultation. A mental health consultant may assist the pastor in developing a program in the local church and community that will enable the church to fulfill its function as a therapeutic community. As an example of such a program, the church could sponsor groups that would involve interaction between persons from different social, economic, and racial groups in order to deal with the broad social issues of our day. It could provide courses on premarital education for the establishment of more stable marriages, discussion groups for mothers of small children, nursery schools for small children, groups for parents without partners, adolescent encounter groups, and other groups with similar purposes. Such groups and others are already in existence in many churches, and mental health consultation would enable these and other such groups to meet the needs of persons in ways that would constitute a program of preventive mental health in the primary stage.

A consultee-centered administrative consultation could provide assistance to the pastor in his problems with the multiple staff and with those lay leaders with whom he must work. It could increase his effectiveness and efficiency in such administration, especially where issues involving interpersonal relationships are concerned. The minister has traditionally been trained to be the only pastor of a congregation. Sharing leadership in a church is always a difficult task to fulfill because of the symbolic meaning of the pastor. It is especially difficult in a church that expresses the concept of a "parity of the ministry," and where there are no clear lines of hierarchical authority. Consultation could help pastors with multiple staffs to work more creatively with interpersonal difficulties within the staff which are bound to occur to some degree. Such consultation could also assist the pastor in his teaching and training function. It could help him to train and equip members of the congregation for their role of ministry to persons involving both educational tasks and assistance with crisis situations.

Secondly, in primary prevention the pastor needs both client-centered and consultee-centered case consultation in order to use his interpersonal skills more effectively. In client-centered consultation the pastor could be assisted not only in his self-understanding but also in the direct service he gives to individuals through his pastoral care and counseling. It could enable him to use his counseling skills more efficiently and to be a more effective counselor. Such counseling effectiveness could make a decisive difference in influencing the outcome of crises and hence provide a significant measure of prevention of emotional disturbance.

In addition, the pastor may be assisted in understanding his involvement in his parishioners' problems. Since the mental health specialist can assist the pastor in understanding himself in his professional role, consultee-centered consultation can provide the pastor with a more secure base for his important involvement with people. Such consultation may be characterized as a primary preventive measure because it enables the pastor to fulfill his occupational role more effectively, and to understand his involvement in such a way as to prevent him from becoming a part of the problem rather than a part of the solution. It will also help him to actualize his greatest potentiality as a care-giver and change agent in the community.

2. Secondary and Tertiary Prevention

The church as an institution and the pastor as a religious leader in the community may also have a role in preventive psychiatry in the stages of secondary and tertiary prevention. This responsibility involves both church and pastor in assisting those in the mental health disciplines in several ways. First of all, the church can take a lead either by initiating mental hygiene clinics in the community and/or in providing specialists in pastoral psychology for comprehensive mental health centers or by staffing pastoral counseling centers. Some churches have established their own mental hygiene clinics with a professional medical, psychological, and social-work team to staff it. Some such clinics have included pastors and specialists in pastoral counseling on the staff whereas others have not. Some community comprehensive mental health centers include pastoral psychologists on their staff. These pastoral psychologists usually divide their time between giving direct service to counselees and providing professional consultation for pastors.

Secondly, as a part of this community responsibility the church could give support and/or leadership in securing the legislation necessary to provide mental health services in a community. At this juncture in the interaction between the two disciplines, the clergy could give real assistance to the mental health specialist in achieving a goal common to both of them. Both professions are concerned with those things which affect persons, and both are seeking some kind of healing for persons in distress and ill health. Hence, consultation at this level could operate in both directions. Each discipline could consult with the other about ways in which the mental health needs of the community can be met.

In terms of tertiary prevention, providing adequate day-care centers for patients released from mental hospitals is an important community need. Now that the mental health specialists can increasingly control mental illness through drug therapy, and it is understood that persons tend to get better faster in the usual environment of normal community life, it is important to return an increasing number of mental health patients to the community. However, this constructive measure is not possible where there is insufficient care for these patients through the provision of community services.

In addition, the church has another important function to fulfill in this stage of prevention. Persons with severe emotional handicaps have a need for the usual relationships in a normal community setting. The church as a community of believers can provide the kinds of teachings and programs conducive to good mental health. As a community institution along with others, it can provide the social resources for a therapeutic community. It could help to form special groups for the special needs of the emotionally handicapped such as those provided by Recovery, Inc.,[47] or it could help to provide the kind of emotional climate within the regular groups of the church in which emotional growth can occur. The consultative services of mental health specialists would be especially important in meeting this community need.

All these measures can express the responsibility of the church for preventive mental health and enable it to fulfill more adequately its own purpose and mission. They can be demonstrated by the churches and pastors, both in the provision of direct service to persons in need, and by using consultative services that will enable them to become more effective care-givers in the community and to become change agents in society, especially in terms of preventing emotional distress and ill health.

Part III

CRISIS INTERVENTION COUNSELING AND PREVENTIVE PSYCHIATRY

Crisis intervention counseling is one of the methods of primary preventive psychiatry, and it is a method that may be adapted for use by pastors in churches. It is a method of preventive mental health because it helps persons to make adaptive rather than maladaptive resolutions of their crises. These responses may be such that not only is the immediate crisis itself resolved adaptively, but a person is enabled to develop his coping abilities so that he will emerge more healthy than he was before the crisis.

Part III examines crisis intervention theory, including the background out of which it developed, the nature of a crisis, and the theory by which an intervention in the crisis is made. The practice of intervention is discussed both from the theoretical perspective and from the application of this practice to its use by pastors.

9

The Theory
of Crisis Intervention Counseling

Counseling persons in crises is nothing new. Counselors have always been called upon in crises. Some counselors are professionally trained for a specific kind of counseling. Others have become counselors simply because they are the kinds of people others seek out or they are in a convenient position where they are sought out because of the unique function of their occupation. Those in the helping disciplines, such as pastors and nurses, are often sought out first because they are the most readily accessible persons in the community, especially in a crisis. They may also be sought out because they are the kinds of persons who are usually sought out in times of crises. An individual discovers that here is a person with whom he can talk.

A pastor is consulted in the event of emotional stress more often than is usually thought. The results (reported in Chapter 3) of the survey conducted in 1960 by the Joint Commission on Mental Illness and Health indicated that 42 percent of the persons with emotional problems reported they had first consulted a clergyman. This percentage is sufficiently high to startle both workers within the mental health disciplines and the clergymen themselves. The relevant question at this juncture is, What happens in such consultations? One important dimension of counseling is examined here, especially in the way it relates to clergymen. The specific aspect of counseling that is being examined is the crisis intervention approach.

BACKGROUND OF CRISIS INTERVENTION

In order to put the crisis intervention approach into proper perspective, a brief discussion of the history of the theory is appropriate. Crisis theory was developed by Erich Lindemann and Gerald Caplan, two psychiatrists at the Harvard University School of Public Health. The theory developed from the Lindemann study in 1943 of the bereavement reactions of survivors of the Boston Coconut Grove fire. Lindemann observed that grief is a necessary and natural reaction following bereavement, and that "grief work" passes through a series of phases. Some persons adapted successfully to the loss after four to six weeks of grief work, whereas others developed psychiatric or psychosomatic illnesses, or experienced abnormally prolonged grief.

Another important contribution to crisis intervention theory came from Col. Albert J. Glass's study of the incidence of combat neurosis, which dealt with the significance of supportive roles. His study indicated that combat neurosis was not so much related to previously existing personality factors in the individuals exposed to stress, but to the circumstances of the combat situation itself. These situational circumstances were related to the intensity and duration of the battle, but more significantly to the degree of support given to the individual by his buddies, by a sense of group cohesiveness, and by the individual's respect for his leaders.

THE DEVELOPMENT OF CRISIS THEORY

The word "crisis" is not used here in the sense of an emergency. A dictionary definition of "emergency" is that it is "an unforeseen combination of circumstances that calls for immediate action." There are various kinds of emergencies in which persons in particular occupations are involved. There are medical and psychiatric emergencies that require the intervention of a medical doctor. There is a specific emergency proposed by the suicidal person which will be examined in Chapter 12. Although the suicidal threat is a kind of crisis, it is a special kind of crisis and requires special treatment in terms of counseling techniques.

Crisis, then, is defined more accurately as the decisive moment, or turning point. It is the culminating point beyond which something crucial happens. It has been defined medically as the point at which there is a change in the disease that indicates whether the result is to be recovery or death. In this same sense it has been pointed out that the Chinese word for "crisis" consists of two characters, one indicating danger and one indicating opportunity.

Interest in the subject of crisis intervention had been aroused by the discovery that in many patients suffering from emotional disorders significant changes in personality development occurred during fairly short periods of crisis. As Caplan indicates: "These transitional points in their history have usually been characterized by acute psychological upset, lasting from about one to four or five weeks, which appear not to have been in themselves signs of mental disorder but rather the manifestations of adjustment and adaptation struggles in the face of a temporarily insoluble problem." [48]

In addition, Caplan pointed out that the history of psychiatric patients often shows that during certain of these crisis periods, individuals seem to have dealt with their problems in a maladjustive manner. Dealing with their crisis maladaptively meant that they emerged from the crisis less healthy than they had been before it occurred. This clinical evaluation is consistent with popular views of a crisis as a turning point in life development, as expressed in the writings of novelists and dramatists. One of the significant aspects of many modern plays and novels is the implication that the outcome is determined by the choices which the characters make in coping with a particular situation.

In some studies of emotionally disturbed patients, Caplan found that although their personalities showed a certain measure of stability at particular phases in their development, they often change suddenly in unexpected ways during periods of crisis.[49] This observation means that crisis periods may be critical times in which constructive changes may take place within a relatively short period of time. Psychotherapists and educators have used this insight in many ways. Personal growth has been stimulated by exposing individuals to situations of increasing challenge and then helping them to discover constructive ways of meeting the stresses.

Caplan's model for crisis theory is based upon the biological concept of homeostasis, by which the physiological processes of the body are maintained in a constant state. Whenever the equilibrium of the body is upset by some deficiency, various processes of the body tend to mobilize to compensate for the deficiency. This process by which the body maintains its own equilibrium was characterized by Walter Cannon as the "wisdom of the body."

Applying this concept of homeostasis to psychological data means that when a person's emotional balance is in disequilibrium, his emotional resources may be mobilized to cope with the problem. In reference to crisis intervention in particular, it is involved with some kind of emotional barrier or hazard. The purpose of the intervention is to mobilize the emotional resources of the individual necessary to cope with the hazard or barrier to his equilibrium. In situations where the hazard is not too much greater than in previous situations, and where a sufficient amount of time is available to deal with it, the individual will be able to cope satisfactorily with it. An "emotionally hazardous situation" occurs when changes in a person's environment take place in which his expectations of himself or his relations with other persons change.[50] Such a change usually involves a loss or threat of loss of some significant relationship. It may be the loss of a relationship through death or separation, the loss of a job with the resultant

loss of self-esteem, the birth of a deformed or mentally retarded child, the loss of a limb, or some type of physically
debilitating illness. The loss or threat of loss may involve
either the normal developmental changes that occur in the
emotional development of a person, or the critical accidental
incidents that may occur in the life of any normal human
being.

However, where the barrier or hazard is larger than usual,
and where there is insufficient time to work out a resolution
to it, a crisis will occur. A crisis results only if the person in
the situation does not have mechanisms available to deal with
it. Coping techniques are required throughout life as the
individual inevitably passes through a succession of hazardous
situations. Certain hazards may result in crises, whereas others
do not. A bereavement experience, for example, may be
handled satisfactorily because the individual has worked out
certain ways to cope with such a significant loss. On the other
hand, it may result in a crisis if it occurs in a new kind of
situation for which no means of coping are available. Such a
crisis, then, upsets the relative equilibrium of this individual,
and he will need to experiment with different ways in which
he can handle it. He may need the assistance of some caring
person to work out a new method of handling the situation.

A theoretical basis for understanding both the danger and
the opportunity of a crisis may be grounded in learning theory.
First of all, no one learns anything when he is on "dead
center," or in complete equilibrium. He learns only when he
is somewhat off-center or in some state of disequilibrium. On
the other hand, if a person is in a position of extreme disequilibrium, the risk may be too threatening for him to learn
any new method or means of coping with a situation. A degree
of security is prerequisite to learning. Everyone needs both
some disequilibrium and some security to explore anything
new.

A crisis, then, constitutes a unique possibility for learning.
It consists of a telescoping of learning possibilities into a

moment of intensity. The intensity of the moment constitutes the danger inherent in a crisis. The radical risk involved may push the individual to retreat into a maladaptive resolution of the crisis and his emotional ability to cope will be impaired. This risk constitutes the danger inherent in the crisis. However, both the state of disequilibrium and the sense of security that develops from the counselor's intervention involve the opportunity for considerable growth within a very limited space of time.

As a person faces problems in his daily life, then, he may develop a state of tension, becoming temporarily upset emotionally. If the situation is not too serious or not very different from other similar situations, and if there is sufficient time and security for him to develop adequate means of coping, the hazardous situation will not become a crisis. However, if the problem confronting the individual is more serious or is unlike anything he has encountered before, and if sufficient time and security are not available to develop some means of coping with it, a crisis will develop and he will need help. Crisis, then, is a term that is reserved for an acute disturbance to an individual as the result of an emotionally hazardous situation. It usually lasts a relatively brief period of time, and in ordinary circumstances is resolved within a period of six weeks.

The Development of a Crisis

Caplan divides the crisis proper into four phases.[51] In the first place, there is the rise of tension of unpleasant affect and some disorganization of behavior following the impact of the hazardous situation. During this phase, the individual is calling upon the usual problem-solving behavior that has worked in the past. In the second phase, if the situation has not been resolved successfully, the tension grows worse. In the third phase, the tension reaches a point where additional internal and external resources are mobilized. At this stage the situation may get better. Emergency problem-solving methods may be used. The problem may be defined in a new way, or certain goals may be given up as unrealistic. In the fourth phase, major disorganization occurs if the problem continues and cannot be solved or avoided.

There are also the normal "developmental crises," as characterized by Erik Erikson. Personality development never proceeds on a straight upward line. Rather, maturing involves gradual stages of development. These stages are punctuated with plateaus, dips, and thrusts forward. Each dip may constitute a challenge. There is both a danger and an opportunity in the developmental crises such as the stages a person moves through from childhood to adolescence, from adolescence to adulthood, etc. When a situation has developed into a crisis in the way the word "crisis" has been defined here, the dip and the danger are greater, but the crisis may also offer a greater opportunity. At the lowest point of the dip, the individual turns to someone for help and the dip may be checked. Progress may be slow at first, but as coping mechanisms are developed, significant progress is made in the maturing process. The significance of the development of a crisis is the telescoping of development. The major changes that may occur in behavior during these periods take place in a relatively short time and may remain stable for long periods of time.

INTERVENTION IN THE CRISIS

Crisis, then, provides both a danger and an opportunity. The model of crisis has been characterized by the stance of a sprinter.[52] While he is standing in a firm position, with his legs apart, planted firmly on the ground, it is difficult to topple him. This stance is likened to the person who is coping satisfactorily with his problem and is in a state of equilibrium. The only trouble is that it is impossible for the sprinter to move from this secure position. When he begins to run he is in a state of physical disequilibrium. He perches precariously on the toe of one foot as he rocks forward to the point where the other foot and leg will take over. At the point of this precarious balance, he can be knocked over easily. His stance is likened to a person in a crisis situation. He may be knocked over easily, which is the danger, but he also has the opportunity of moving forward. At the very point of crisis, a slight influence, then, may produce a great change quickly because the person is in a precarious and painful disequilibrium. In such a time of crisis the intervention of other persons such as a pastor or counselor can significantly affect the outcome for the better. Within this concept of intervention, the first six weeks are crucial.

In addition, the outcome of the crisis is not determined simply by previous experiences. The outcome may be more crucially influenced by unique psychological and situational factors. The solution to the problem and the new equilibrium reached by this solution may be more adequate or adaptive than what had been achieved previously. The changes that take place or the new methods of coping that are developed may be more adequate than any previous coping skills in meeting future stressful or hazardous situations. In other words, a person who successfully resolves his crisis will tend to be more healthy emotionally than he was before the crisis occurred. Intervention at the time of crisis suggests that a minimum of action at this juncture provides a maximum possibility of change. Counselor assistance at such a decisive moment presents the possibility of a significant change in the direction of recovery.

Gerald Jacobson distinguishes between the intervention in a crisis and other forms of psychotherapeutic intervention. He has characterized crisis intervention theoretically by a diagram representing the sum total of a person's functioning.[53]

The shaded area of Figure 4 represents the stable or relatively stable part of a person's functioning, including his basic attitudes, values, and commitment. It includes his relation to

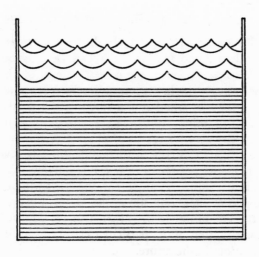

FIGURE 4

reality factors including both his inner reality (intrapsychic) and his relations with others (interpersonal). It refers to the characteristic (characterological) way a person behaves. It involves the behavior that makes a person recognizable as the same individual throughout his lifetime.

The thin fluid area on top of the solid area represents those aspects of a person's functioning which are changing from time to time. All of us are in the process of change, and the fluid area represents this part of one's functioning. In a situation of stress, a person may experience mild anxiety or depression until he develops some way of dealing with the new situation. In a crisis, the fluid area is enlarged and the ratio of the fluid to the solid area is changed significantly. In this case the individual confronts a crucial turning point in his life. When his previously developed means of coping are not adequate to the new situation, he will be upset during the period of time in which he is experimenting with a number of different solutions. The new solutions may be adaptive or maladaptive.

Regardless of the way it is resolved, the crisis does not continue, usually, beyond four to six weeks. During the four to six weeks from the onset of the crisis the level of anxiety becomes increasingly high, but usually diminishes after that period regardless of whether the resolution was adaptive or maladaptive. In other words, if the situation is not faced realistically, the person's level of functioning is impaired and he will be less able to cope with reality. An adaptive resolution will help the person to deal constructively with similar situations in the future. In any event, the crisis will be resolved within a period of about six weeks. The only question is whether the resolution is a constructive or destructive one, both in the situation of the particular crisis and in relation to similar situations in the future.

10

The Practice
of Crisis Intervention Counseling

The goals and methods of crisis intervention have been worked out by the staff of the Benjamin Rush Center for Problems of Living. They have used some of Caplan's theories as well as those which have been worked out in their own practice.[54]

GOALS OF CRISIS INTERVENTION

The new idea that is basic to the crisis intervention approach is that a person is often most able to make significant progress in the midst of a crisis if certain interventions can be made by the counselor. The nature of these interventions needs to be understood and plans need to be made for them. In a general sense there are four basic goals of crisis intervention that may be applied to pastoral care and counseling.

First of all, there is a need to assist the person in crisis to look into himself as quickly as possible. Since a person usually sees a counselor within a period of one to three weeks after the onset of a crisis, it is important to help him get into contact with himself as soon as possible. He needs to become sensitive to his most highly charged emotions, thoughts, purposes, and conduct as soon as possible after the crisis has been triggered by some specific event. The purpose of intervention at this point in the counseling is simply to encourage the expression of buried feelings. In a crisis such as bereavement, feelings of hostility and guilt may be repressed. Supporting the person's expression of negative feelings will assist him in reestablishing contact with his own intense feelings. The expression of such negative feelings does not mean blaming others for his predicament but is simply a matter of facing all the feelings that have occurred in the experience of the crisis.

A second goal in the crisis intervention approach is to oppose any further regression of the person in a crisis. The individual is either totally or partially immobilized in the midst of a crisis, and he tends to regress. He wants the counselor to free him from the conflict between facing and evading reality. Although he has ambivalent feelings about it, he tends to want someone to take care of him. The crisis intervention counselor actively assists such a person in facing up to the reality of the situation and hence opposes any further regression. The counselor holds up constructive actions and adult standards to him. In helping the individual to face the problem realistically, the counselor discourages any further infantilization or dependence upon him. In confronting the individual tactfully with the reality of the situation, the counselor is saying that he will not do anything for the person that he can do for himself. Supporting him and resisting regression, he can begin to regain some hope of influencing the outcome, and his self-confidence may be strengthened. He may begin to see how he can change the direction of the crisis.

A third goal of the counselor is to assist the individual in becoming an observer of himself in the immediate here and now of his crisis. The present situation needs to be objectively reviewed with him. The individual not only needs to look at his situation realistically; he also needs to understand as much about it as possible. Learning about the facts of a situation increases one's power over it. Once it is understood, it is no longer as frightening as it has been. The goal is to assist the individual in experimenting with different methods of coping with the crisis, thus increasing his self-confidence in relation to the crisis situation.

Finally, the counselor needs to help the individual in crisis by opening up the channels of communication to other helping persons. These persons may be relatives or friends who are in a position where they may continue to be supportive of the individual. Other professionals of the helping disciplines such as pastors and nurses may also have a helpful function to fulfill at this point. The person in a crisis who acknowledges that he needs help has already begun the first step. Since one way to avoid reality is to deny any need for help, such an acknowledgment indicates the development of the necessary means to cope with the crisis. Such an acknowledgment of need also involves the pastor and the community of care in a continuing supportive role. Such support does not protect the individual from the reality of the situation, but it does provide a sense that he is not alone. He knows that others are standing alongside him in his difficulty.

The Methodology of Crisis Intervention

The methodology of crisis intervention is always involved in attempting to mobilize the inner resources of the person in crisis. The crisis intervention counselor approaches a problem of crisis from the perspective of normality. Instead of allowing or encouraging regression, the counselor encourages the individual in crisis to see his problem as a normal one. He encourages the individual in mobilizing his own ego resources to cope with whatever problem has triggered the crisis.

One way to approach the actual practice of crisis intervention is to divide the separate steps into two stages.[55] The first stage involves the basic function of exploration of the various aspects of the crisis situation itself. The second stage involves the work of problem-solving. It consists of the exploration of alternative ways of solving the problem posed by the crisis.

Stage 1

In the first stage, the counselor is directed to explore the actual situation confronting the person in crisis. In some situations the exploration may be simple. The identification of a death in the family as a precipitating event may be a relatively simple matter. However, in many situations the precipitating event is not readily accessible to the person in crisis. He may be convinced that the occasion of his divorce has precipitated the crisis, when in reality it may be something else. At any rate, the precipitating event is not necessarily what the individual presents in the first place. Furthermore, an individual in crisis often cannot identify any event at all as the precipitating factor.

Since the individual will tend to defend himself against the experience of the pain occasioned by the precipitating event, it may remain below the level of consciousness. Indeed, the focus of most interventions in any counseling or psychotherapy is the defense against recognizing and experiencing the particular experiences that have been painful. In outlining the steps that he may take in planning intervention in the crisis, the counselor begins by identifying the actual event which has precipitated the crisis. He needs to be able to identify this event for his own sake, first of all. Directed questions are a helpful tool to uncover this event. What is threatening to him? What is new in the ongoing situation in this particular crisis? What is the immediate problem as differentiated from the characterological problem?

Secondly, in view of the fact that the individual will defend himself against the experience of pain occasioned by the precipitating event, the counselor will need to be able to identify the defensive maneuvers the individual is using against his recognition of such an event. Again, the counselor will need to be able to identify these defensive maneuvers and to understand some of their meanings before he will be able to interpret this data to the person in crisis. The counselor will need to describe the chief or most powerful defenses the person is using against recognizing and feeling his response to them. Again, questions may be directed to the person in crisis that may help both the counselor and counselee to discover the defense mechanisms. In what ways does this particular situation seem to be different from other similar situations? Who are the significant persons related to the crisis, and how are they involved?

Thirdly, the counselor will need to listen for previous situations in the individual's life that are similar to the present crisis experience. He will need to understand just how this situation differs from similar situations in the past, and how this difference is related to the individual's defenses. If the counselor can relate the uniqueness of this crisis event to the defenses the counselee is using against experiencing it, he will be able to interpret how the counselee is warding off his responses to this event. If he has faced similar problems in the past, he may have developed means of coping with them that could be used in this crisis. The counselor will need to ask how such problems have been faced in the past.

Fourthly, the counselor will need to discover just why the person cannot cope with this situation as he has in previous situations. What new impasse has been brought about by this new situation? When the counselor discovers the reason why the individual can no longer use the same means of coping with the problem, he will be able to understand the dynamics of the situation. Formulating the dynamics of the situation for himself will enable the counselor to understand more clearly the nature of the present impasse.

Fifthly, the counselor needs to state the problem to the counselee in clear, concise terms. At this point it is a matter of the counselor's intervention in the midst of the crisis. It is an intervention that describes the situation as clearly as possible. The counselor needs to share with this individual the basis of the conflict that he is experiencing. Such knowledge will increase the person's sense of power over the situation. To the degree that he understands the crisis event, he will begin to regain some hope of influencing the outcome of its course.

Finally, the counselor will need to help the individual to confront the crisis situation in manageable doses. Persons usually need some kind of relief from having to look at the whole of reality at one time. No one is so strong as to be able to look at any severely threatening reality without some relief. In addition, if these interventions have not been successful, the counselor will need to go back and explore the reasons why they were not.

Stage 2

This stage consists of problem-solving behavior. First of all, the counselor is directed to explore alternative ways of solving the problem posed by the crisis. Different ways of solving the problem may be worked out in collaboration with the counselee. In working out some means of coping with the problem, the counselor will need to review the various problem-solving methods that were used in the past in similar situations. Some of these previous coping mechanisms may have been maladjustive in the sense that the individual emerged less healthy after the hazardous situation than before. An analysis of such problem-solving behavior will assist the counselor in working out more adjustive means of coping with the crisis situation.

Finally, it is important to note that learning how to cope with a crisis will not necessarily help to solve long-standing characterological problems. For this reason, the counselor must be prepared to help the parishioner to consult with other professionals when the need is indicated by the following factors: (a) evidence of need for emotional understanding in terms of long-range goals; (b) clear-cut motivation for additional therapy; (c) the availability of mental health resources and the necessary financial ability to pay for the therapy.

Two Approaches to Crisis Intervention

In their attempt to understand the varied uses of the crisis intervention technique, Gerald Jacobson and his associates differentiated between what they have labeled as the generic and the individual approaches.[56]

1. *The Generic Approach*

The central thesis of the generic approach is that for each crisis there are certain identifiable patterns of responses. Some of these responses result in an adaptive and others in a maladaptive resolution of crises. There are certain crises such as bereavement, divorce, change in body image, etc., that have identifiable patterns of responses. In the generic approach there is no attempt to determine or assess the specific psychodynamics of the individual involved in the crisis. Rather, the focus of this type of intervention is on the course that a particular kind of crisis characteristically follows, and a corresponding treatment plan aimed toward an adaptive resolution of the crisis.

Intervention consists of specific measures designed to be effective for the target group as a whole. Approaches will include direct encouragement of adaptive behavior, general support, environmental manipulation, and anticipatory guidance. This broad approach has many similarities to public health measures of a preventive nature, such as immunization. This generic approach is especially relevant to the type of crisis intervention that may be carried out by persons not specifically trained in the mental health field. This methodology will be elaborated upon in the next chapter as the crisis intervention approach that may be most often used by the pastor. Since no special training in the psychodynamics of personality is required for this type of intervention, its use is readily accessible to the pastor in his counseling work.

2. *The Individual Approach*

The individual technique is characteristic of the therapeutic approach used in crisis intervention clinics such as the Benjamin Rush Center. Of course, both generic and individual approaches are used, and they are mutually complementary. The individual approach differs from the generic in its emphasis on the assessment by the mental health professional of the specific intrapsychic and interpersonal processes of the individual. This information may not always be directly interpreted to the counselee, but the psychodynamic material needs to be understood by the therapist. This approach differs from long-term or extended psychotherapy because it is not involved with the characterological or long-established psychodynamic processes except as they provide clues which may aid in the understanding of the current crisis. "The focus clearly is on why and how a previous equilibrium had been disturbed and on the processes involved in the reaching of a new equilibrium." [57]

Another differentiation from more conventional counseling therapy is the frequent reference to both family members and significant other persons related to the individual in crisis. Unlike generic techniques, the individual approach to crisis intervention requires a greater measure of psychological understanding on the part of the counselor.

Although pastors may not ordinarily use the individually tailored approach, two case histories are presented here for comparison with those histories included in the next chapter on the generic approach. They involved persons seen by the author in a church pastoral-counseling center. The names and circumstances have been changed to protect the anonymity of the counselees.

Case History No. 1

Beth was twenty years old and unmarried. She was not in school at the time but had graduated from high school a few years before. She had previously held a job as a clerk in a store but had now withdrawn from any activity whatsoever and simply stayed at home. When she was seen for the first time she was a very withdrawn and frightened person. Her mother brought her to the counselor because she was concerned about the radical change in her daughter, her withdrawal into herself as well as her hostile responses. Although Beth was an attractive young woman, she began by complaining that she was ugly and that she would never attract a man because of her ugliness. She complained especially about the structure of her face saying that her eyes were too small and so close together, and that it was altogether an ugly face. She kept insisting that no one could help her because the structure of her face and the position of her eyes could not be changed. As a result of her feelings of hopelessness, she was apathetic about life. She was not motivated to leave her room or to go out and get a job, and she had very little interest in life. The first intervention consisted simply of permitting the verbalization of her negative feelings about herself and accepting these feelings as hers. As she talked, she revealed that she had previously had plastic surgery on her nose about three years before. She had felt good about the results. She had not had any counseling at that time. An intervention at this point consisted simply of encouraging her to talk about this change in her body image, and how she felt about herself. Since she had not had sufficient opportunity to explore her feelings about this change in her facial appearance, she had not learned an adaptive means of coping with her original feelings of ugliness about her nose.

When the counselor intervened with questions about her experiences during the past two or three weeks, she revealed that her boyfriend had broken off with her about two weeks prior to this appointment, and that she had begun to withdraw after that. Although she had been dating several times a week, she had not had any possibilities of a date for more than two weeks. She felt she was not sought out for any dates because of her ugliness, and that she would never have a chance for another such relationship. In the course of the questioning she related that her mother and father were divorced, and that she had visited her father about three weeks previously. It was just before her boyfriend broke off their relationship.

She talked about how she resented her mother and how close she had felt to her father. When the counselor questioned her about the visit, she told about her father's new family since he had remarried. She related that she had felt somewhat out of place, and that her father's attention was directed primarily toward the children in his new marriage. She felt largely ignored, and then her boyfriend had told her he didn't want to see her again.

Intervention at this juncture consisted of encouraging her to verbalize her feelings about being hurt in both situations, and these feelings were both accepted and interpreted. It was interpreted to her that she had suffered rejection in both situations. Her need for acceptance by her father had been accentuated by her boyfriend's rejection. When she had experienced rejection in the past, she had used the excuse that her nose was ugly. She had not developed any means of coping with the rejection but had evaded it by turning to her feelings of ugliness. Surgery on her nose had robbed her of the use of this means of coping with her feelings. Now she "discovered" that her eyes were so small and close together that her face was ugly, but in a way that could not be changed. Hence, no one could help her because no one could change the structure of her face. She was now confronted with the problem of rejection, but not in an examination of her characterological problem of her relationship with her father which was broken at a crucial point in her psychosexual development by the divorce. She was confronted with the possibility of discovering other ways to cope with her feelings of rejection and lack of popularity with young men. Additional intervention involved experimentation with job interviews and additional social contacts as well as examining her limited patterns of interest and involvement with others which made her a less interesting person.

In this intervention, some psychodynamic understanding was necessary in order to relate the experiences of rejection of this particular person to the crisis she was experiencing. At the same time, there was no attempt to work with her characterological problem which would in all likelihood continue to distort the nature of her relationships with men. Intervention was limited to the crisis situation. The goal was to help her develop an adaptive means of coping with this particular crisis which had immobilized her to the extent that she was unable to function. The counseling extended over six weekly sessions and enabled her to gradually examine her feelings about her body image, her limited pattern of interests and interpersonal conduct, and her emotional needs in relation to the present crisis confronting her.

Case History No. 2

Phil was about twenty-eight years old, single, and had been working as a cook in a restaurant. He came to the counselor after having been almost completely immobilized for about two weeks. About two weeks before, he had walked off his job in the restaurant. He had not indicated a desire to terminate employment, but had simply not returned to work. He had not given any reason for leaving, but each day had indicated only that he could not return to work. During the first few days he was sick in bed with physical symptoms. After a few days he felt able to get up, but he still stayed in his room most of the time and never left the house. He still felt he could not return to his job even though he could no longer use his physical symptoms as an excuse.

He had finally come in for counseling at the insistence of friends from whom he rented a room. He began by talking about his job and his feelings about not being able to return to his job. In his responsibility as cook, he had several persons working under him. It was the first time he had been given such responsibility, and he did not feel capable of coping with it. To compound the problem, his anxiety was increased by a highly authoritarian chef under whose direction he worked. Exploring his reactions in previous positions, he indicated that in the past when he could not cope with such an authoritarian boss he had simply walked off the job and secured another. This reaction, then, was his way of coping with such a hazardous situation in the past.

The first intervention involved questioning about what was different or new about this situation. Why did his previous means of coping not work in this situation? What was different here? It did not seem to be a different kind of situation except that this chef had reminded him of his father. He was aware that he had resented his father, and that he had never worked out a basis for a relationship with him. He was aware that he simply could not return to the job because of these feelings. However, he could not figure out why he was unable to seek out another job as he always had in the past, and why he found it difficult even to leave his room and the house in which he lived. As he talked about his situation in general, it became evident that he was renting his room from a couple who had befriended him years before and to whom he felt deeply indebted. In addition, this couple had gone to some trouble to assist him in securing this particular job which involved greater responsibility and a higher salary than he had ever before earned.

It soon became clear that in leaving this job he felt guilty about leaving a position secured for him by his friends who had become parent substitutes for him. The conflict between his inability to work under a "bad father" and his fear of rejection by the "good parents" was more tension than he could handle, and he became literally immobilized. Fearing that he would appear ungrateful to them, he was unable to indicate that he would either terminate his job and seek another or return to his position. His inner conflict made it impossible for him to move in either direction. He became immobilized.

The first intervention consisted of describing this data to him. The relationship between the authoritarian chef and his father, and his usual means of coping with his tensions were described. The relationship between his images of the couple who had befriended him and the good parents that he needed was pointed out. This material was described in the context of his previous means of coping, and why this conflict made it impossible to work in this situation. In addition to describing this data to him, emotional support was given to the possibility of seeking another job. Additional interviews could have enabled him to explore different job opportunities. However, following the second interview he called to inform the counselor of the job he had secured just three days after the last session. He had gone out on two job interviews and had secured the second position.

It is clear that his characterological problems were not a part of the counseling with this individual. He had not worked out his problems with authority figures, but he was enabled to function adequately enough to move out of an immobilized state and secure a position. Although he obviously needed at least some psychotherapy, he demonstrated that he was not ready for any referral for additional psychotherapeutic work. Hence, even though he had not solved his characterological problem, he had returned to a level of functioning that was at least as capable as before the crisis. Since he had been able to talk over the matter with his parent substitutes, it may be inferred that his means of coping with this crisis was an adaptive one which increased his coping skills in general.

SUMMARY

It will be clear from these discussions that the individual approach to crisis intervention involves an understanding of the psychodynamics, or emotional basis, of human behavior. However, this approach does not attempt to work with the characterological, or characteristic, ways a person deals with his problems. Hence, it is different from long-term psychotherapy.

The individual method is also different from the generic approach to crisis intervention, which will be discussed more fully in the next chapter. In addition, the individual approach is not necessarily a long-term involvement. It is still a method of crisis intervention, and as is evident in the last case history, it may consist of only two sessions. Hence, it is not the length of the counseling work that is important but the approach which is needed for a specific purpose.

Regardless of the specific approach used, some guidelines developed at the Benjamin Rush Center may be helpful to the counselor in understanding the dynamics of the crisis. These approaches are complementary and the counselor with psychodynamic understanding and counseling skills will use both of them. The counselor may direct these questions to himself as he concludes the first interview. They may be used both to provide guidelines for the conduct of the sessions and/ or for the evaluation of the sessions.

1. What recent loss, threat of loss, or other hazard has occurred in the person's life, especially in the past two or three weeks?
2. What are the symptoms of the crisis that have developed from this hazard?
3. What long-term problem areas are being reflected in the current crisis?
4. What are the previously utilized coping mechanisms that are no longer effective?
5. What are the potential mechanisms that may be used in working with the crisis?
6. Who are the significant persons in the individual's life who may be used in achieving successful resolution of the crisis? [58]

11

The Pastor's Use
of Crisis Intervention

The particular use to which crisis intervention will be put depends, of course, upon the training and skill of the individual counselor or therapist. Although pastors vary in the degree of such training and skill, most of them do considerable counseling utilizing at least the first two levels of crisis intervention.

FOUR LEVELS OF CRISIS INTERVENTION

The staff of the Benjamin Rush Center have developed what they call four levels of crisis intervention. The first two levels are common to pastoral counseling and have been developed elsewhere.[59] A brief treatment has been included here simply for the sake of review. The third level of intervention is elaborated upon here because it is the new approach that would be most readily used by pastors in the process of their regular pastoral care and counseling. The individual level has been included in the previous chapter primarily for the sake of the clinically trained pastor.

1. Supportive or Nonspecific Level of Intervention

Perhaps the supportive role in counseling is the one most widely used by pastors. Involvement in simple human interaction is basic to pastoral care. In reference to crisis counseling in particular, the technique consists of nonspecific forms of intervention. It involves, first of all, simply listening carefully. At a time when this art has been largely lost, it is important to begin with careful, disciplined listening. This practice is the basis of any valid counseling, and it fulfills a particularly important function in the pastor's supportive role. When the pastor responds to a parishioner's crisis by simply "being there for him" he is using his own self to intervene in the crisis. Such intervention can also communicate some possibility of hope in influencing the outcome. Such hope may be understood simply through the expression of caring in the encounter itself.

2. *Environmental Manipulation as Intervention*

Environment manipulation may also be important for counseling in general and for crisis counseling in particular. Intervention to remove some hazard or to change some objective circumstance is an important level of such counseling. It may be especially important in situations involving the problem of poverty or of the cities' ghettos. Such manipulation may include assistance in securing a job or in changing a community political situation that is fraught with hopelessness. In instances of the generic level of crisis counseling, environmental intervention may fulfill an important function. These instances will be examined further below.

3. *The Generic Level of Crisis Intervention*

The general theory of crisis intervention has been introduced in Chapter 9. Such intervention may be defined as any action that a counselor may take in his effort to influence the course of a particular crisis. His purpose is to assist the individual to discover a more adaptive means of coping with both the present and future crises.

The specific thesis of the generic approach is that for some types of crises, there are certain identifiable patterns of responses. The theoretical issues involved with this approach have been developed by Dr. Jacobson and his associates.[60] They have made a helpful differentiation between the individually tailored approach used by the trained psychotherapist and this approach which may be more readily used by the pastor in his counseling work. Since no special training in the understanding of the psychodynamics of personality is required for this type of intervention, its use is especially relevant for persons not specifically trained in the mental health field.

The basic thesis of this approach is that in crises involving some significant loss, there are certain identifiable patterns of response. In crises such as bereavement, divorce, loss of health, or birth of a defective child, there are patterns of responses that ordinarily occur. This approach is particularly well documented in the work of Erich Lindemann on bereavement. He discovered that a bereaved person goes through a well-defined process of adapting to the death of a loved one consisting of so-called "grief work."

Since there is no need to assess the psychodynamics of personality in this approach, the focus of any intervention is on the course that a particular kind of crisis characteristically follows. Hence, intervention consists of specific measures designed to be effective for the target group as a whole. Intervention in the counseling sessions would be determined by the process of the particular type of crisis. Although the counselor would need to be sensitive to the highly individualized way a person experiences a crisis, he would not need to be trained in the diagnosis of personality dynamics in order to choose the proper ways to intervene.

The pastor's choice of the kind of intervention, then, will be influenced by the characteristic course of a particular crisis. His plan for working with an individual will be aimed toward an adaptive rather than a maladaptive resolution of the usual process of a particular type of crisis. His approach to intervention will include, first of all, the general supportive measures of any good counseling. Careful listening by a person who shows some evidence of caring will help to give an individual some sense of hope that this crisis, too, will pass. Such listening will be an encouragement to him to express his feelings, many of which may have been buried and unavailable to his conscious awareness.

In addition to careful listening, the counselor will directly intervene in a way to assist the person in crisis to look into himself and to get into contact with his most highly charged emotions, thoughts, purposes, and conduct. The counselor will assist him in becoming an observer of himself, especially in relation to the "here and now" of the crisis in which he finds himself. The counselor will review the present situation objectively with him, but this review will not necessarily be made all at once. No one is so strong that he can meet all the aspects of a crisis at once. Hence, he will be helped to confront the reality of the crisis gradually and in manageable doses. In review of the person's situation, the counselor may also help him to learn certain facts that may help him regain some hope of influencing the outcome of the crisis.

Thirdly, the counselor will encourage the individual in working out some adaptive solution to the crisis. His acceptance of the crisis as something that could happen to any normal person encourages the counselee to discover an adaptive rather than a maladaptive way of coping with his present crisis. The counselor will assist the individual in experimenting with different methods of coping with the crisis, and the efforts he makes toward adaptive behavior will be supported. These efforts may include learning more facts about the situation which will give the counselee hope of influencing the outcome. Resisting regression and dependency, the counselor will assist the individual to examine these facts and any constructive action which he might take. In other words, the counselor does not do anything for him that he can do for himself.

In experimenting with various alternative actions, the counselor may choose to intervene through some form of environmental manipulation. Such manipulation may include changing one's job, moving out of a home, or going to school. It involves making some change in the social and/or physical surroundings in order to develop a more adaptive way of coping with a crisis. It may involve experimentation with various changes in order to develop an adaptive means of coping.

Another type of intervention in the generic approach to crisis resolution has been referred to as anticipatory guidance. Since the counselor knows the general course of the crisis, he can anticipate some of the counselee's responses. As Dr. Jacobson once pointed out, anticipatory guidance is like seeing a cliff ahead and directing the individual's attention to it.[61] Of course, it is obvious that some persons would deny that any such problem (cliff) exists. And some will actually have to come face-to-face with the problem (cliff) or will become overwhelmed by the problem (fall off the cliff). The counselor's function in every instance is simply to offer to stand by when any of these responses occur. He is offering his availability to the individual as he confronts the various stages of the crisis. Such an offer of support will enable the individual to call more readily upon the counselor for help in coping with his feelings when they occur as well as when they seem to be overwhelming.

CASE HISTORIES

Examination of some illustrative case histories may be helpful in elaborating upon this approach to crisis intervention. The names and other identifying material have been altered or omitted in order to preserve the identity of these individuals who were counseled in the context of a church counseling center. The commentary following each case presentation will discuss the kinds of intervention the counselor made in the

process of counseling. Case histories have been chosen to illus-
trate several kinds of crises and the characteristic course of
these crises. The crises chosen for presentation here are the
ones most likely to be encountered by the pastor.

Case History No. 1—Bereavement

Bill was a man sixty years of age who had been notified less
than a week before that his son had been killed in Vietnam.
He attended church regularly and his religious faith seemed
to be meaningful to him. He was a simple man, but a genuine
human being who had just suffered a severe loss. He was a
high school graduate. Since his faith was important to him, his
turning to the church was a natural step.

He was very depressed and apathetic when he came in. He
began by revealing that his son had been reported killed in
action and then went on to talk of the family. His wife had
died just two years earlier and his only other child, a daughter,
was not close to him. She was married and lived in a distant
city, and had not maintained much of a relationship with
him. He did not feel close to her. Although he had been
closer to his friends in the church than to his daughter, he had
withdrawn from some of his activities in the church following the death of his wife. Initially, then, he was saying that
he had been miserable, and now that his son had been killed
there was nothing worth living for. He had not been eating
regularly and had not been sleeping well since receiving the
tragic news. He continued to express his negative feelings
during this interview, and they were accepted. Intervention
during this first interview consisted of simple encouragement
to talk about his son. Talking about the son seemed to effect
an initial relaxation of his intense depression, and a date
and time were set to get together during the next week.

During the second session Bill began to show some guilt
feelings about not having been a good enough father to his
son. There were things he wished he would have done with

him. During this session he asked about going into the sanctuary. Seeing the counselor as pastor as well as counselor, he asked for prayer and kneeled as the counselor prayed with him. During the encounter of this session he seemed to accept more readily both the reality of his son's death and of his own feelings of loneliness.

In the third hour he began expressing anger against the government and finally against God for having allowed his son to be killed, and also for allowing his wife to die. He was visibly relieved that his anger was accepted and to be reassured that it was normal to have such hostile feelings. It appeared that he had not allowed himself to voice these feelings at the time of his wife's death, and that he was now completing some unfinished "grief work." His hostility was both accepted and clarified as a normal feeling for such a time. Indeed, an intervention was made by simply encouraging him to express these feelings and by clarifying that God was certainly more interested in hearing his honest angry responses than in any silencing of his feelings. During this session he also began talking about his previous withdrawal from active involvement in the church. Another intervention consisted of exploring his participation in a particular group in the church to which he had referred earlier in the session.

His final session was two weeks later. He talked about many things during this hour, including some of the feelings he had experienced earlier. However, the major thrust of the session was his talking about the church group that he had attended since the last session. He had renewed some acquaintances and they were generally supportive of him in his crisis.

These four sessions took place in a period of about six weeks. The progression of this crisis may vary from person to person, but the course of bereavement usually includes the following pattern of responses according to Lindemann: (1) some somatic distress or complaint; (2) preoccupation with the image of the deceased; (3) guilt feelings; (4) hostile reactions; and (5) loss of one's usual pattern of conduct.[62] It may be observed that this particular person may have been responding to some unfinished "grief work" in relation to his wife's death two years previously. However, the progression of his bereavement followed a typical pattern, and an understanding of the course of the crisis provided the basis for the counselor's specific interventions.

These interventions consisted of encouraging him to talk about the deceased, accepting and encouraging the expression of negative and hostile feelings, accepting guilt feelings, and using the religious resource of prayer as an adaptive form of behavior to cope with them. Finally, encouragement to reestablish a relationship with a group at the church opened up some channels of communication with persons who could provide some needed emotional support. This intervention may also be characterized as environmental manipulation in the sense that he was encouraged to make a change in his usual activities in order to develop a more adequate means of coping with his situation. In Bill's case, it may be more accurate to say that he was encouraged to reactivate a pattern of conduct which he had discontinued after the death of his wife. The number and types of intervention will vary from person to person, but they tend to follow the course of the crisis itself rather than being predominantly related to the personality dynamics of the individual. The interventions did not take into account any of the characterological problems of the individual but simply directed him back to the "here and now" of his present crisis.

Case History No. 2—Divorce

Grace was a woman of thirty-eight who had been married for about fifteen years. She had three children, from ages of seven to eleven. Her husband had, in her words, come home one night about two weeks before and, entirely unexpectedly, stated that he wanted a divorce. Since then he had actually consulted an attorney and she had secured legal advice for herself. According to her, the announcement came as a complete surprise. However, as she talked she realized that there had been times when she had wondered about what was happening to her marriage. In the first interview she became increasingly aware of the distance that had developed during the previous few years, especially during the previous two years.

In the second and third interviews she began to express negative and hostile feelings. Her husband's business had demanded extended periods of time away from home and she became aware that he paid very little attention to either her or the children even when he was home. She was able to verbalize her feelings about his neglect of the children. Two of their children had asthmatic conditions and one was serious enough to necessitate hospitalization. She was able to both accept these feelings which she had buried and to express them toward her husband. She also became aware that she had given up any hope of establishing a really open and growing relationship with her husband.

During the next few interviews she began to express an increasing amount of hostility toward her husband. She began to blame him for everything that had happened. She recalled that when she had accused him of neglecting her and the children while he was home from a business trip, he quarreled angrily with her. She withdrew from the quarrel, and he ended up spending even more time away from them. An intervention at this time consisted of interjecting that a relationship always involves two persons and that she would need to examine what kind of "payoff" or "reward" she got from withdrawing from the quarrels. While reflecting on the fact that they had not had any real quarrels for about two years, she became aware of the kind of compromise she had made simply to keep some kind of peace and stability in the marriage. She began to see how much his anger threatened her and that she had accepted his withdrawal as an easier solution to her own anxiety about the relationship.

Although she continued to express anger toward her husband in the next few interviews, she began to examine what problems she had brought to the marriage. When she began to blame her husband and feel sorry for herself the counselor intervened to confront her with her own responsibility to be fully herself in the relationship.

During the sixth session the counselor's intervention consisted of exploring with her some constructive steps that she would need to take. These steps involved the need to secure a job and sell her house which she could no longer afford to keep. As she began to cope with these very concrete tasks she began to express some hope for herself and her children.

The increased ego strength which she gained through the discovery that she could take care of herself enabled her to begin to examine some of her long-buried guilt feelings in relation to her children. She began to see that she had chosen to stay with her children instead of spending time with her husband in his hobbies and sports interests. She discovered that she had not been a companion to her husband in some ways because of her overprotection of her children. At the same time, she experienced some feelings of rejection of her children. Interventions by the counselor involved acceptance of her guilt feelings and support for her increased awareness of her own responsibility for the break in the relationship with her husband.

Interventions in the seventh through the ninth sessions consisted of additional support as she applied for a part-time job to supplement her income and as she worked to get her house ready for sale. Other interventions included the suggestion that she reexamine her relationship with a women's group at the church which she had discontinued at the time of the divorce and that she look into the possibility of the organization Parents Without Partners. By the time of the ninth and final session she was experiencing some support from this new group and had developed a friendship with a man who had the care of two children from his divorce.

In the first two interviews Grace seemed to be seeking some understanding for the cause of the divorce, but in reality she was gradually working toward the acceptance of the fact of the divorce. One intervention at this juncture was to assist her in accepting the reality of the separation and in coming to this awareness gradually and in manageable stages. Another intervention was the acceptance of, and encouragement to express her negative feelings.

Interventions during the second and third interviews consisted of support for the expression of her hostile feelings toward her husband which she had successfully suppressed, and in some instances repressed to the extent that she had actually forgotten she ever had such feelings.

During the next few sessions the counselor interventions consisted of breaking up her "game" of blame and self-pity. She was confronted with her own responsibility for the relationship and the way she had evaded quarrels in order to "keep peace." His anger had been more threatening than his withdrawal, and hence, she compromised her responsibility for the relationship.

Her coping with the very constructive steps of securing a job and selling her home increased her ego strength to the point where she could begin to examine some of her buried guilt feelings. They involved a pattern of overprotection of her children in order to compensate for her guilt at resenting them for interfering with the time she could have spent with her husband. Hence, this pattern involved her in choosing to stay with them rather than going off with her husband at times when he could have been with her.

Her increased acceptance of her own responsibility for what had happened to the relationship and the support she experienced from both the counselor and her new friends in Parents Without Partners enabled her to take full responsibility for herself and her children in their new life together. There was no attempt to work with the characteristic ways she dealt with her dependency problem, but her behavior was adaptive in this instance and her acceptance of her responsibility for herself showed considerable growth in her ways of coping with such a situation.

A divorce is a typical disruptive experience and may be illustrative of other types of experiences such as a broken engagement, a terminated affair, or a broken relationship with a friend or member of the family. Such a disruptive experience has something in common with bereavement and may, at certain points, be akin to grief work. It is the person grieving for the significant loss that he has experienced. Although each individual experiences a divorce in his own way, there are patterns of responses that occur in most instances similar to this one. At least this pattern of responses may occur in cases where a disruptive experience is initiated by one of the parties in the relationship over the objections of the other. All the parts of this pattern would not necessarily be present in all situations. Nor would the order in which they occurred be repeated. However, the similarities evident in numerous such situations enable the counselor to understand the usual course of such a crisis.

Case History No. 3—Miscarriage

Jane was twenty-four and had been married for about a year to a man five years her senior. He was a very stable person who offered her both love and security. She was seen about three weeks after her miscarriage. She had reacted at first with deep disappointment, but for the past two weeks had become increasingly upset, apathetic, and depressed. Her husband became concerned about her increasing apathy, and she finally realized her need to seek help when she kept feeling worse. Her friends had encouraged her not to talk about the miscarriage and kept reassuring her that she would get over her disappointment and feel better very soon. She felt free to consult the pastoral counselor at a church counseling service because of her religious convictions.

She began talking about the disappointment she felt. She and her husband had been very happy when she learned she was pregnant. Her husband was especially happy and had talked about elaborate plans for their first child. Now she felt guilty that she had let her husband down. Early in the first interview she talked about an abortion that she had secured several years prior to her marriage. The first intervention concerned the acceptance of her feelings of guilt about her abortion and encouragement to talk about these feelings.

At this point it seemed to be important to her that she was talking to a counselor related to the church. There were some elements of confession in the session, and forgiveness was expressed both in the acceptance of the counselor and in an interpretive intervention pointing out the nature of God's forgiveness. Although it did not seem to be a predominant theme, her feelings of guilt were related somewhat to the fear that this was God's way of punishing her for the abortion, and a subtle fear that it was an indication that she would never be able to have a baby. Since her guilt feelings were related to this fear, the interpretation of forgiveness was related to the intervention indicating that this miscarriage did not in any way indicate that future pregnancies would result in miscarriage. It was suggested that she talk with her physician about it also, but she was relieved to hear this supportive word.

In the second session, which was the final one, she expressed grief for her unborn fetus. Although she was not aware of having had fantasies during her earlier pregnancy, she had numerous fantasies about this one, especially in relation to the love she had for her husband. She was now grieving for the loss of one who was the product of their love. Acceptance of her grieving feelings, both in the sense of their being normal and in the understanding of the pain which she experienced, was important to her. Her grief work seemed to relieve her and she expressed no desire to make another appointment.

In a miscarriage the woman has suffered a significant loss. The course of the crisis usually includes some physical complaint, feelings of apathy and depression, guilt and grief. There may also be considerable hostility. Jane's hostile responses were primarily related to her guilt feelings over the matter of the abortion, which were, in reality, hostile feelings directed against herself. Again, although the experience of a miscarriage has highly individual meanings, there does appear to be a usual course for such a crisis.

Case History No. 4—Mental Retardation and Birth Defects

Betty was twenty-five, a college graduate, married, and lived in a small town near the city. She had delivered her first child about eight weeks prior to her coming in for counseling. She explained that about three weeks before her counseling appointment, her family physician had informed her and her husband that their baby was a mongoloid child, even though it was a borderline case. She was now staying with her parents in the city where she had taken the baby for some medical checkups with specialists at the suggestion of her physician. She had received a definitive diagnosis about ten days prior to her counseling session.

She was depressed and somewhat apathetic. She began talking about her reason for coming to the city. The session with the doctors ten days previously had destroyed any hope she had for good news. The first intervention was simply encouragement to talk about her feelings. She revealed that after the birth of the baby she had shown him off proudly to her friends. When the family physician finally told her the truth, he confessed that he had been aware of the situation from the first but simply could not bring himself to tell her the truth. She was encouraged to express her feelings, and she talked about the trauma of hearing the first word of it from her physician. However, she had not let herself think much about it until the specialists had examined the baby. Now she lived with her grief for her child. Her feelings of grief were accepted and she began to express hostile feelings, especially toward her family doctor who had not had the courage to inform her of his original diagnosis. She expressed bitter feelings against God, who allowed such a thing to happen. These feelings were accepted and supported by interpreting that God was concerned with her honest feelings.

She indicated that her parents and friends had urged her to put the child in an institution for the mentally retarded. She expressed some guilt feelings for desiring this solution, and she seemed most apathetic when she talked of it. She seemed to assume that since her family physician, parents, and friends had all urged her to place her child in an institution, there was no other solution. However, she began talking of taking care of her child, and another intervention was to encourage her to talk about this and to explore the possibility of such a plan, contrary to what seemed to be everyone's advice. Almost immediately she began to express some aliveness. As she was encouraged to explore other possibilities, she began to appear brighter, increasingly alert, and more interested in her future. Another intervention consisted of encouraging her to learn more about the occurrence of mongoloid births, and pointing out the fact that there was no reason to believe that the remainder of her children would not be normal. Being reassured that such births occur erratically seemed to give her increased hope of influencing the outcome of her crisis experience.

The course of this crisis consists of depression and apathy. The depression appears to be related both to grief and to hostile feelings which have not yet been expressed. Apathy seems to be related to feelings of hopelessness. Supporting this individual in the expression of grief and hostility, and increasing her knowledge about the situation, enabled her to have an increasing hope of influencing the outcome of the crisis. There appears to be a similar course to the crisis situation in which various kinds of birth defects occur. The problems for parents of children with birth defects will, of course, be different if they are physical rather than mental defects, but the initial reaction to the event of the birth seems to be quite similar.

Case History No. 5—Body Image

Joe was about twenty-six years old, unmarried, but engaged to be married in a few months. He was a high school graduate and was working for the railroad when he lost both legs in an accident in the railroad yards. He was seen in the hospital less than a week after the accident at the request of both his doctor and his family. He was very depressed and apathetic. He had a religious background. Although his immediate family had not said anything about it, some relatives and friends were implying that the accident was the way God tested a man.

In an initial intervention he was encouraged to talk about how he felt about himself. It was difficult for him to get in touch with his feelings, but as his negative feelings were accepted he began to express some hostility. He slowly began to express feelings of hostility toward the railroad, God, and his relatives and friends who had suggested that somehow God was involved in his predicament. As he became increasingly free to cope with his hostile reactions, he was reminded of his responsibility for himself.

As he became more able to talk about his physical condition, he seemed to be adapting to his new situation gradually but painfully. He began to talk about his missing legs in a way akin to grieving. He expressed feelings that can only be interpreted as grief for his lost limbs. He was encouraged to express his hostile and grieving feelings, but the focus of the intervention was upon the constructive steps he might take in order to cope with life with such a handicap.

In conjunction with the physical therapist in the hospital, new information was imparted to him regarding the possibilities of artificial limbs, and just what steps would be necessary to train him to walk again. Interventions also included consideration of some occupational therapy in the hospital and vocational rehabilitation which would enable him to retrain for a new kind of job.

The focus of these interventions was upon his gradual awareness of the reality of his new situation, his hostile and grieving feelings, and the constructive steps that he could take in order to cope with life under the new and difficult circumstances of a serious physical handicap. The gradual awareness of the extent of his physical handicap was a part of the crisis process and was completed in six sessions. After his release from the hospital, however, he was seen for about twenty additional weeks during which time he worked with the gradual acceptance of his new body image. Such therapeutic work on the acceptance of body image could be a part of any therapy with a person who has a physical handicap, but it would usually involve crisis intervention only in situations where some significant loss had been recently experienced.

Case History No. 6—Role Confusion

George was twenty, single and enrolled in his second year of college at the time he came in for counseling. Prior to his coming to a large city to attend college, he had lived in a small town in the north. He had established himself in high school as an excellent model builder and had won significant recognition in several different instances for his models of spacecraft. He had been an excellent student in his science courses in high school.

He came to counseling initially because of his failing grades in college science courses. Since his academic record had been excellent in the past he could not understand his present feelings of apathy or his academic failure. He had begun to feel anxious and fearful at the beginning of the school year in which he was now enrolled. In probing to discover whether or not something had happened within the past few weeks, the counselor discovered that George had been classified as

I-A by his draft board about five weeks previously. His student deferment had been set aside because of his grades and he had now been reclassified. Although his lack of motivation to study had begun about six months prior to the draft notice, he had begun to experience panic about the time of the draft classification.

During his first and second years in college he had been attempting to discover the direction of his career. He had not been able to make any final decision about his occupational role, and the possibility of the draft exerted additional pressure upon him to decide immediately. When this pressure became intolerable, he would drive up into the mountains where he would hike the trails by himself. The threat of the draft had become a difficult situation, but the actual draft classification caused a crisis to occur. He knew that once he was drafted into the armed services his freedom of choice and movement would be curtailed. Since the draft meant that he could no longer participate meaningfully in decisions involving his own goals and intentions he began to experience apathy in his studies. The actual draft classification climaxed the deprivation of freedom and resulted in panic, and before his second counseling session he had developed an ulcer. Unable to cope adaptively with his "role confusion," he developed a maladaptive means of coping. Although the development of the ulcer successfully eliminated the problem posed by the draft, it was a maladaptive resolution of his personal crisis.

This case is not typical of a person in an identity crisis. Work with this young man involved some psychodynamic understanding of his personality structure. Briefly, he had both a strong need to be dependent and a need to control his environment. He was able to express these needs both through his model-building and his effective means of escape to the mountains. However, this case illustrates both the intensity of the role confusion and the *necessity* for discovering a resolution to the crisis.

First of all, the age of this young man illustrates the problem of role confusion. During the crucial years of late adolescence and early adulthood, the individual is confronted with the problem of choosing his values and discovering who he is in terms of the role he has to fulfill in life. Erik Erikson has indicated that during these years a person is in danger of role confusion. He may be unprepared to determine just what his role is to be in life. Undue pressure, such as the arbitrary fact of the draft, may involve him in a panic reaction of flight from both the necessity of making such a choice and the psychic inability to do so at the specific time dictated by an arbitrary deadline such as a draft classification.

The necessity for some crisis resolution is made evident by the rather dramatic somatic effort in the development of an ulcer. The body reacted to the psychic threat by offering a resolution to the crisis. It happened shortly after the first counseling session and during the sixth week following the receipt of the draft classification. Not every young man of this age and in this circumstance will react with the same panic, but any such person could be confronted with a similar crisis of role confusion. He will need time to explore his choice of values and goals with some degree of freedom. These values and goals may be expressed through the various commitments including the choice of career, education, and marriage. Intervention will include the exploration of these life choices in a way in which the individual has some sense of power and influence over his destiny.

LIMITATION OF THE GENERIC APPROACH

There are some factors that limit the application of the generic approach. First of all, there are many types of crises that have not been sufficiently studied. It is impossible to outline the characteristic patterns of adaptive or maladaptive resolutions to these crises because they have not yet been identified.

A second limitation is true of the formation of any pattern

involving human responses. Persons experiencing a crisis common to other human beings will usually respond with their highly individualized meanings. As human beings, we share both an immense sense of commonality among all men and a high degree of individuality. Persons with some particular kinds of personality dynamics may not respond according to a characteristic expectation.

Since every experience is filled with personal meaning, no two similar crises will follow precisely the same course. Nevertheless, there are the *usual* patterns of responses for particular crises. When the counselor interventions do not seem to be successful, other experimentation will need to be made. In the event that interventions continue to be unsuccessful, and the individual seems to continue in the same state of apathy or depression, it will be necessary to consult with a mental health specialist or to refer the counselee for a more individualized type of intervention, and/or for a more traditional treatment of his chronic and characterological problems.

12

The Pastor and Suicide Prevention

Counseling with persons who are either suicidal or potentially suicidal is a specialized instance of crisis counseling and requires a specific type of intervention. Suicide prevention is an important area in which the pastor may have special significance along with other care-givers in society.

Since suicide usually occurs to a member of a family, suicidal clues may become apparent to the pastor as he works with families. In addition, since the large majority of persons with emotional problems consulted a pastor first of all, he may have special importance in suicide prevention. Suicide often occurs in conjunction with the normal and accidental life crises, therefore the pastor's involvement with persons during these times provides him with an additional opportunity. He is called upon professionally on the occasion of normal crises such as birth, marriage, and death. He is often consulted in the accidental crises such as sickness, divorce, or separation.

Suicide is a problem of society as a whole, and the various care-givers in the community will need to cooperate in using each other's resources. The pastor may become pivotal in such a cooperative effort. The church may provide both the social resource of a community institution and its specific religious resources in meeting the problem of suicide prevention.

The Problem

Suicide is a serious national problem. Although it is usually considered within the context of mental health, it is a human problem that affects more than twenty thousand families a year. Another way to put it is that once every minute someone tries to take his own life, and sixty or seventy times each day these attempts succeed. Even these figures are not accurate because many suicides are not reported as such. The stigma attached to suicide and the problems it raises for families means that many so-called "accidental deaths" are, in reality, suicides. In addition, many deaths that result from actual accidents may be traced to unconscious desires to take one's own life and hence may be the actual cause of the "accident."

Those who are knowledgeable about this human problem estimate that it is becoming increasingly serious. Medical statistician Louis I. Dublin was quoted as saying to a meeting of physicians in Los Angeles: "It would not be rash to estimate that perhaps as many as 2,000,000 individuals are now living in our country who have a history of at least one unsuccessful attempt at self-destruction. A great many will try again. On the basis of a recent study, 10% will ultimately succeed. I emphasize this fact in order to impress the huge size of the problem with which we are involved and to focus attention for a need for a more concerted effort on the part of socially-oriented groups to attack this problem seriously." [63]

It is estimated that among people ages fifteen to fifty, suicide is the fifth leading cause of death. Its toll is greater than "the combined deaths from typhoid fever, dysentery, scarlet fever, diphtheria, whooping cough, meningococcal infections, infantile paralysis, measles, typhus, bronchitis, malaria and rheumatic fever." [64]

In addition, a team at the Harvard Medical School under the direction of Dr. Alfred L. Mosley has been quoted as saying that on the basis of their study, suicides are a "significant though unknown" proportion of the 48,000 annual auto deaths in the United States.

In addition to understanding the immensity of the problem, there are some additional facts about suicide that may be helpful to the pastor. It is estimated that twice as many men as women commit suicide, although twice as many women make the attempt. The rate of suicide increases as age increases, and men over fifty have the highest rate of all. Adolescents may commit suicide on impulse, but they are not the most serious area within the problem as a whole. Although the rate has increased recently, 1960 statistics indicate that only about 4 adolescents for each 100,000 of the population commit suicide, whereas about 55 per 100,000 of those over fifty commit suicide. Additional data is included in *The Cry for Help*, a definitive work on suicide that may be a helpful resource for understanding the various dimensions of the problem.[65]

SOCIO-PSYCHODYNAMIC UNDERSTANDING OF SUICIDE

People commit suicide for all sorts of reasons. There is no single causative factor. Indeed, a suicidal impulse may be thought of as a symptom that something is wrong. It is up to the diagnostician to discover just what has gone wrong and what can be done about it. In addition, there are various ways to classify the suicidal attempts. The reader who is interested in a more specific study of the psychodynamics of suicide is referred to Part II of *The Cry for Help* referred to above. Discussions from the perspectives of Freud, Jung, Adler, Harry Stack Sullivan, and Karen Horney are included along with other approaches.

The sociological classification of Durkheim, which was originally published as *Le Suicide* in 1897, is the most frequently quoted means of classification.[66] Although it was not available in English until 1951, this classification has shown a remarkable durability. His designation of *altruistic* suicide refers to a willingness to give up life because of a disciplined commitment to a group or cause which is greater than the person's own interests. *Egoistic* suicide refers to the choice which a person could make because the organized group to which he belonged allowed for decisions on the basis of individual responsibility. *Anomic* suicide refers to those situations in which a person's relation to his social group is radically changed and in which he has experienced some significant loss. By *fatalistic* suicide Durkheim refers to factors of excessive regulation such as slavery.

The chief merit of a sociological classification is that it examines the relation of the individual to the group with which he identifies. Such examination takes note of the significant influences upon a person's life. A psychological analysis of suicide may provide a basis for understanding such psychodynamic constellations as hostility, dependency, anguish, hopelessness, shame, paradoxical striving, and others.

Edwin Shneidman has attempted to synthesize the sociological position with its emphasis upon the "social fact" with a psychological understanding of the conflict within the individual. "A synthesis between these two lies in the area of the 'self,' especially in the ways in which social forces are incorporated within the totality of the individual. In understanding suicide, one needs to know the thoughts and feelings and ego-functionings and unconscious conflicts of an individual, as well as how he integrates with his fellow men and participates morally as a member of the groups within which he lives." [67]

Although he does not claim that his classification encompasses all the necessary dimensions, Shneidman does propose that all committed suicides may be viewed as one of the following three types: *egotic, dyadic,* or *ageneratic.* He attempts to synthesize the important elements of "the intra-psychic stress, the interpersonal tensions, the strained ties with groups, idiosyncratic modes of thought, inner pain and hopelessness, and even one's role in the family of men." [68] Such a synthesis is especially relevant to the concept of crisis intervention and it relates to the way a pastor may use his interventions in suicide prevention most helpfully. These three types are discussed briefly along with some suicide notes which provide helpful illustrations.

In this classification *egotic* suicide refers to what is happening within the individual. It is the intrapsychic conflict. It is psychological in nature and the effect of the environment is secondary. Relationship to others is not the primary consideration in his suicidal thoughts. He is responding to himself and his feelings about himself. Suicide becomes the annihilation of the self or the destruction of the ego. He is saying, "As far as life is concerned, I've had it." He wants out of life because of his fears, confusions, pain, etc. Examples of *egotic* suicide notes are as follows:

(from a thirty-one-year-old single male)

Mr. Brown:
When you receive this note, call the police.
Have them break down the door panels of the cabinet nearest the window in room 10. My body will be inside. Caution—carbon monoxide gas! I have barricaded the doors shut so that if for any reason the guard becomes suspicious and tries to open the doors, there will be enough delay to place me beyond rescue.

It seems unnecessary to present a lengthy defense for my suicide, for if I have to be judged, it will not be on this earth. However, in brief, I find myself a misfit. To me, life is too painful for the meager occasional pleasure to compensate. It all seems so pointless, the daily struggle leading where? Several times I have done what, in retro-

spect, is seen to amount to running away from circumstances. I could do so now—travel, find a new job, even
change vocation, by (sic) why? It is <u>Myself</u> that I have
been trying to escape, and this I can do only as I am
about to!

Please take care of a few necessary last details for me.
My residence is—100 Main Street.

My rent there is paid through the week.

My only heirs and beneficiaries are my parents. No one
else has the least claim to my estate, and I will it to my
parents.

<u>Please break the news to them gently</u>. They are old
and not in good health. Whatever the law may say, I
feel I have a moral right to end my own life, but not
someone else's.

It is too bad that I had to be born (<u>I</u> have not brought
any children into this world to suffer). It is too bad that
it took me more than 31 years to realize that I am the
cause of whatever troubles I have blamed on my environment, and that there is no way to escape oneself.
But better late than never. Suicide is unpleasant and a
bother to others who must clean up and answer questions, but on the whole it is highly probable that, were
I to live, it would cause even more unpleasantness and
both to myself and to others.

Goodbye.

Bill Smith

(from a forty-seven-year-old married male)

Mary Darling,

My mind—always warped and twisted—has reached
the point where I can wait no longer—I don't dare wait

longer—until there is the final twist and it snaps and I spend the rest of my life in some state run snake pit.

I am going out—and I hope it is out—Nirvanha, I think the Bhudaists (how do you spell Bhudaists?) call it which is the word for "nothing." That's as I have told you for years, is what I want. Imagine God playing a dirty trick on me like another life!!!

I've lived 47 years—there aren't 47 days I would live over again if I could avoid it.

Let us, for a moment be sensible. I do not remember if the partnership agreement provides for a case like this—but if it doesn't and I think it doesn't, I would much prefer—I haven't time to make this a legal requirement—but, I would much prefer that you, as executrix under my will, do not elect to participate in profits for 2 or 3 years or whatever it may be that is specified there. My partners have been generous with me while I worked with them. There is no reason why, under the circumstances of my withdrawal from the firm, they should pay anything more.

I could wish that I had, for my goodby kiss, a .38 police special with which I have made some good scores —not records but at least made my mark. Instead, I have this black bitch—bitch, if the word is not familiar to you—but at least an honest one who will mean what she says.

The neighbors may think its a motor backfire, but to me she will whisper—"Rest—Sleep."

Bill

P.S. I think there is enough insurance to see Betty through school, but if there isn't—I am sure you would out of the insurance payments, at least—

I hope further and I don't insist that you have the ordinary decency—decency that is—to do so—Will you see Betty through college—she is the only one about whom I am concerned as this .38 whispers in my ear.

(from a twenty-one-year-old single female)

12:00 p.m.

I can't begin to explain what goes on in my mind—its as though there's a tension pulling in all directions. I've gotten so I despise myself for the existence I've made for myself. I've every reason for, but I can't seem to content myself with anything. If I don't do this or some other damned thing, I feel as tho I'm going to have a nervous collapse. May God forgive me, and you too, for what I am doing to you, my parents who have always tried so beautifully to understand me. It was futile, for I never quite understood myself. I love you all very much.

Mary[69]

A *dyadic* suicide is related to the significant other person or persons in one's life. It involves the experience of a radical change or loss in relationship to a significant other person. Hence, such a suicide is primarily social or interpersonal in nature. It involves saying something to another person, and the suicidal act is usually an expression of hostility directed toward the significant person in his life. Examples of this type of suicide note are as follows:

(from a thirty-five-year-old single male, who committed suicide after he killed his girl friend)

Mommie My Darling,

To love you as I do and live without you is more than I can bare. I love you so completely, whole-heartedly without restraint. I worship you, this is my fault. With your indifference to me; is the difference. I've tried so hard to make our lives pleasant and lovable, but you didn't seem to care. You had great plans which didn't include me. You didn't respect me. That was the trouble. You treated me like a child. I couldn't reach you as man and woman or man and wife as we've lived. I let you know my feelings toward you when I shouldn't have. How I loved you, what you meant to me. Without you is unbearable.

This is the best way. This will solve all our problems. You can't hurt me further and anyone else. I was a "toll" while you needed me or thought you did. But now that I could use some help, you won't supply the need that was prominent when you needed it. So, good bye my love. If it is possible to love in the hereafter, I will love you even after death. May God have mercy on both our souls. He alone knows my heartache and sorrow and love for you.

Daddy

(from a sixty-six-year-old divorced male)

Mary:

We could have been so happy if you had continued to love me. I have your picture in front of me. I will look at it the last thing. I do love you so much. To think you are now in the arms of another man is more than I can stand. Remember the wonderful times we have had— kindly—Good bye Darling. I love you, W. Smith

Your boy friend Pete Andrews, is the most arrogant, conceited ass I have ever known or come in contact with.

How a sensible girl like you can even be with him for 10 minutes is unbelievable. Leave him and get a real fellow. He is no good. I am giving my life for your indescressions (sic). Please don't let me pay too high a price for your happiness. All your faults are completely forgotten and your sweetness remembered. You knew I would do this when you left me—so this is no surprise. Good bye darling—I love you with all of my broken heart.

W. Smith

(from a thirty-eight-year-old divorced female)

Bill,

You have killed me. I hope you are happy in your heart, "If you have one which I doubt." Please leave Rover with Mike. Also leave my baby alone. If you don't I'll haunt you the rest of your life and I mean it and I'll do it.

You have been mean and also cruel. God doesn't forget those things and don't forget that. And please no flowers; it won't but mean anything. Also keep your money. I want to be buried in Potters Field in the same casket with Betty. You can do that for me. That's the way we want it.

You know what you have done to me. That's why we did this. It's yours and Ella's fault, try and forget that if you can. But you can't. Rover belongs to Mike. Now we had the slip and everything made out to Mike, he will be up after Rover in the next day or so.

Your Wife[70]

Ageneratic suicides are related to Erikson's use of the word "generativity" in referring to the concern of one generation for the next. It is involved with a person's loss of a sense of belonging to his history or to his generation. He has lost his sense of belonging to a larger whole. Such a suicidal person has experienced a sense of alienation from the basic family or cultural group to which he belongs, and he experiences a sense of "interpersonal impoverishment." Hence, *ageneratic* suicide may be considered primarily as sociological in nature. It may also be perceived as religious in the way it is related to familial, cultural, national, or group ties which give meaning and value to one's life. Examples of this type of suicide are as follows:

(from a forty-three-year-old divorced male)

TO WHOM IT MAY CONCERN,
AND THE AUTHORITIES:

You will find all needed information in my pocket book. If the government buries suicides please have them take care of my body, Navy Discharge in pocket book. Will you please seal and mail the accompanying letter addressed to my sister whose address is: 100 Main Street.

My car is now the property of the Jones Auto Finance Co. (You will find their card in my pocket book). Please notify them of its location. You may dispose of my things as you see fit.

W. Smith

P.S. The car is parked in front of the barbershop. The gear shift handle is broken off, but the motor is in high gear and can be driven that way.

Dear Mary,

The fact of leaving this world by my own action will no doubt be something of a shock, I hope though that it will be tempered with the knowledge that I am just "jumping the gun" on a possible 30 or 40 years of exceedingly distasteful existence, than the inevitable same end.

Life up to now has given me very little pleasure, but was acceptable through a curiosity as to what might happen next. Now I have lost that curiosity and the second half with with its accompaniment of the physical disability of old age and an absolute lack of interest in anything the world might have for me is too much to face.

The inclosed clipping seems to tell it much better than I.

My love to both you and mamma, for what it's worth.

Sorry,

Bill

(Clipping)

The question, then, as to whether life is valuable, valueless, or any affliction can, with regard to the individual, be answered only after a consideration of the different circumstances attendant on each particular case; but, broadly speaking, and desregarding its necessary exception, life may be said to be always valuable to the obtuse, often valueless to the sensitive: while to him who commiserates with all mankind, and sympathizes with everything that is, life never appears otherwise than as an immense and terrible affliction.

(from a fifty-year-old single male)

TO THE AUTHORITIES:

Excuse my inability to express myself in English and the trouble caused. I beg you not to lose time in an inquest upon my body. Just simply record and file it because the name and address given in the register are fictitious and I wanted to disappear anonymously. No one expects me here nor will be looking for me. I have informed my relatives far from America. Please do not bury me! I wish to be cremated and the ashes tossed to the winds. In that way I shall return to the nothingness from which I have come into this sad world. This is all I ask of the Americans for all that I had intended to give them with my coming into this country.

Many thanks.

Jose Marcia

(from a fifty-eight-year-old married female)

I have been alone since my husbands death 14 years ago. No near relatives.

I am faced with another operation similar to one I had ten years ago, after which I had many expensive treatments.

My friends are gone and I cannot afford to go through all this again. I am 58 which is not a good age to find work.

I ask that my body be given to medical students, or

some place of use to some one. There will be no inquiries for me.

Thank you.

(from a sixty-one-year-old divorced female)

You cops will want to know why I did it, well just let us say that I lived 61 years too many.

People have always put obstacles in my way. One of the great ones is leaving this world when you want to and have nothing to live for.

I am not insane. My mind was never more clear. It has been a long day. The motor got so hot it would not run so I just had to sit here and wait. The breaks were against me to the very last.

The sun is leaving the hill now so hope nothing else happens.[71]

THE PASTOR'S ROLE IN SUICIDE PREVENTION

In addition to the dynamics of suicide presented above, there are some other facts about suicide which may be of assistance to the pastor. Paul Pretzel, of the Suicide Prevention Center in Los Angeles, has pointed out three of these facts.[72]

First of all, there is the factor of *ambivalence*. The fact that most persons have mixed feelings about wanting to die makes the concept of suicide prevention a possibility. It is an error to assume that a person has a wholehearted desire to die. Hence, the function of the pastor is to relate to that part of the person's ego which wants to live. Although his desire to take his life must be taken seriously, and he must be heard, there is still that spark of life which can be strengthened.

Secondly, suicidal feelings give evidence of a *crisis*. A suicidal act is often an impulsive act. Although some suicidal persons are chronically so, most persons can be helped if they are heard in the midst of crisis. Clinical experience has shown that if a person is assisted during a particular crisis, the chances are good that he will not attempt suicide again. Indeed, of those persons who have already attempted suicide, only about 10 percent will actually succeed in later attempts.

Finally, there is the attempt of the suicidal person to *communicate* something to someone. This has been characterized as the "cry for help." It represents the attempt of the individual to communicate with a significant other person or with the world-at-large. According to the experts in suicide prevention, nearly every suicidal person gives a cry for help before he actually attempts suicide. In situations where suicide has been successfully executed, "psychological autopsies" have been conducted. These autopsies have consisted of interviews with persons close to the deceased, examining just what had been communicated before suicide. In nearly every instance some kind of cry for help was given and the clue was either not identified as such or was not heeded.

There are specific ways in which a suicidal person communicates his intention. They may be interpreted as signs or warning signals. There are the *subtle suicidal hints*. There is a hint of deeper meaning in comments such as, "Life is no longer meaningful to me," or "I don't see anything worth living for anymore." *Suicidal threats* are to be taken seriously. It used to be said that if a person talks about suicide, he will never go through with it. This assumption is absolutely incorrect. Persons who threaten suicide often carry through with it. A *suicidal attempt* is always a dramatic cry for help. If the significant other persons in his environment have not heard his cry, he may attempt it again. Anyone who expresses himself through certain types of symptoms may be giving nonverbal cues. Sudden change in an individual's life, such as a change in personality or in the kinds of activities in which he has participated, are always danger signals. Long and painful physical illnesses, chronic sickness, sudden or chronic depression, loss of appetite, difficulty in sleeping, sudden change in the degree of alertness in physical or mental activity, sudden withdrawal, feelings of worthlessness and self-recrimination are all danger signals that merit some kind of supportive response from the pastor. In addition, there is an inherent danger in any crisis in which a significant loss is experienced. This loss may be the loss of a significant other person through death or separation, or the loss of self-esteem through financial or career changes.

In working with suicidal persons, the pastor will need to use some of the methods of crisis intervention. He will need to listen carefully and give evidence of his caring. Talking frankly with the suicidal person, the pastor will need to help him in examining his feelings and in exploring his suicidal plans with him. Discussing the individual's suicidal plans may assist him in getting in touch with his most highly charged emotions, thoughts, and goals, and it will not be detrimental to him. The suicidal person wants to be taken seriously and to be understood. Such an open discussion will not mean the pastor condones his intention, but he should not speak of suicide as an immoral act. Such a judgmental attitude may block the possibility of further communication and the individual's need to communicate may be the basis of his suicidal intention in the first place. Understanding an individual's ambivalence toward suicide may provide the basis for the pastor's identification with that part of the individual's personality which seeks to live. The pastor may be supportive of the suicidal person. He may enable him gradually to accept some of the unfortunate aspects of his reality in a way that he can cope with it satisfactorily and adaptively.

Secondly, the pastor can make an active effort to relate the suicidal person to others in his environment who may be helpful. These persons may include members of the family, friends, or simply persons within the church or community who would care for him. They might be professional persons providing specialized care or they might simply be warm and accepting human beings who care for others.

Thirdly, since suicidal impulses have been identified as a failure in trust, the pastor may assist the suicidal person to reestablish the sense of trust in others and in God. The pastor has access to the religious resources of a tradition as well as the potentially therapeutic resources of a social institution. Both may be used constructively with a suicidal person, especially if he has had a background in a religious tradition.

In addition, Shneidman's classification of suicide may be used profitably in conjunction with the theory and practice of crisis intervention. Although no principle can be uniformly applied, his helpful guideline could be used by the pastor. In instances of *egotic* suicidal impulses it would be especially important for the pastor to direct the individual to a mental health specialist if it is at all possible. Psychodynamic understanding of the individual would be especially important in such an instance of intrapsychic disturbance.

However, in cases of *dyadic* or *ageneratic* suicidal feelings, the nature of the pastor's relationship and his available resources may be used very effectively in suicide prevention. Although psychodynamic understanding of the individual would be helpful in all instances, the nature of these suicidal phenomena seems to be social. These phenomena may also be basically religious in the sense that a person's values and commitments are involved. A person's values are related to his sense of identification and that in turn is related to the group to which he is committed. A person's sense of *being* is involved in his relationship with both significant other persons and with the group that gives him some sense of historical roots. Belonging to a church or synagogue means more than simply belonging to that particular organization. It means belonging to the history of a particular people with particular values. It is a sense of belonging to the ages. In recognition of the basic religious nature of this identification, a pastor may fulfill the need of the suicidal person to relate symbolically both to the significant other persons in his life and to the group that can give him a sense of belonging to a particular people with a particular history.

In many ways clergymen have a unique function in relation to suicide prevention. They are readily available for consultation and are normally sought out in times of crises. They are the only professional persons who may call in the home without some specific reason and hence early warning signals may be noted. Pastors also work with families and with separate family members in the normal course of their work. A wife who makes a remark about the sudden development of her husband's mood of depression is giving a subtle signal to the pastor that something may be seriously wrong. The pastor may perform a crucial preventive function by assisting members of this family in communicating with each other and in being supportive of each other in a time of potential crisis. It is also possible that the husband unconsciously hopes his wife will notice something is wrong and hence that she will assist him in receiving some professional help from the pastor or others in the helping professions.

In addition, the clergyman has access to the resources of a community institution that may fulfill certain preventive and therapeutic functions. Programs sponsored by the church can provide resources to facilitate better communication between husband and wife, and between parents and children. Program assistance can be provided to assist persons in developing mentally healthy life-styles, to prepare for career development and career changes, and to help prepare persons for retirement and for the constructive use of their leisure time. Furthermore, both individuals and groups within the church can be trained to fulfill the therapeutic function of caring for persons suffering some kind of deprivation. Fulfilling a supportive function to the person suffering from separation or loneliness or pain may prevent the development of a suicidal or other type of crisis.

As the leader of a religious community, the clergyman also

has access to the specific religious resources available to that particular community of believers. Some concept of hope is a part of most religious traditions. The loss of hope is a critical factor in the dynamics of suicide. A loss of hope will be especially critical for persons in their fifties and sixties, and may be the most important factor in the heightened risk of suicide in persons over fifty years of age. At any rate, the religious resources of hope may be an important resource in suicide prevention, and the pastor's work with persons in this age group may fulfill an especially critical need.

13

A Psychology of the Community

It is not exactly startling to suggest that significant developments are taking place in the area of community mental
health. Several years ago, M. Brewster Smith suggested that
we are involved in a mental health revolution. He indicated
that there had been two prior revolutions in the mental health
movement. The first one was involved in releasing persons
from an alienation from society by the designations of sickness
and the establishment of mental hospitals. The second revolution came about through the influence of dynamic psychiatry,
of which the chief spokesman was Freud, and the developing
profession of psychoanalysis. "Now the third revolution throws
off the constraints of the doctor-patient medical model—the
idea that mental disorder is a *private* misery—and relates the
trouble, and the cure, to the entire web of social and personal
relationships in which the individual is caught." [73]

Any practitioner in the area of mental health knows that
both the prevention of emotional pathology and the development of a sound mental health for individuals within *any*
social milieu demand an integrated effort of the total community. The community can no longer charge a particular
profession with the responsibility for developing the mental
health of the community; nor can a specific profession lay
sole claim to such a responsibility. Rather, it behooves the
community as a whole to develop a psychology *of* the com-

munity that will foster the principles of sound mental health and provide the basis for the actualization of human potential.

Developing a psychology *of* the community involves both commitment and a coordinated effort of the natural care-givers in society with those equipped to provide psychological expertise to meet these human problems. From the perspective of the minister, priest, or rabbi, it involves a religious dimension of commitment. Regardless of the specific dogma or patterns of beliefs, this commitment relates to what happens to man. The clergyman is related to the historic development of pastoral care in his *healing, sustaining, guiding,* and *reconciling* ministry. These traditional pastoral functions form a coherent *whole* in relation to a ministry to the community as a *whole*.

Although the clergyman knows that the chief function of the church or temple is *not* simply to provide the direct service of counseling, he is directed to meet human need through his healing, sustaining, guiding, and reconciling ministry. He also knows that his ministry is not limited to a particular segment of the community. The medical model of psychoanalysis and individual psychotherapy meets the needs of the middle and upper classes, but it is the poor, the uneducated, and the "poor treatment risks" who have the really serious mental health problems. Both the clergyman and the mental health professional encounter these people, and those in either profession know that something is radically wrong when the most needy segment of society receives the least attention and the most ineffectual treatment.

From the perspective of the mental health specialist, the development of a psychology *of* the community involves a broadening definition of therapeutic activity. A recent statement from within the profession of psychology emphasizes this concern. "The concept of community psychology seems particularly to be receiving increasing support as a necessary direction for the practice of psychology. The phrase, 'community psychology' typically elicits the notion of medically oriented inpatient-outpatient mental health programs. Such programs are an important part of the movement toward community mental health. However, the effective practice of psychology must move beyond this limited concept. As Brayfield suggested, the ideal program should find expression among the major social arenas of the community, such as schools, courts, *churches* [my italics], business, and industry. The trend, then, is toward involvement in social action programs which transcend the traditional definition of community mental health. . . . The emerging role of the community psychologist, then, can be seen as that of a consultant who may direct his expertise to other professionals in a community health effort or to any of a broad range of persons, or problems, at a variety of levels within society." [74]

Hence, the mental health specialist increasingly sees himself as offering his skills as they relate to the needs of society. More and more he sees his role as a consultant at a variety of levels and in a multiplicity of directions that is not limited to the specific functioning of the community mental health center. In this role he becomes a translator of psychological knowledge. He translates psychological data into a community-oriented service. This translation involves consultation and paraprofessional training for those professionals in the community who encounter human problems and crisis situations in the normal course of their work.

The nature of such a collaborative program of preventive mental health constitutes a "calling." This work is a calling for both the clergyman and the mental health professional. It is a calling to meet human need with a preventive program relevant to the complexity of both the nature of mental health and the stresses in contemporary society. It is a calling to work together to develop a psychology *of* the community that will both protect those who are endangered by emotional stresses, and enhance the potential of human beings through the development of sound mental health.

Notes

1. Seward Hiltner, *Preface to Pastoral Theology* (Abingdon Press, 1958), pp. 89–172.

2. William A. Clebsch and Charles R. Jaekle, *Pastoral Care in Historical Perspective* (Prentice-Hall, Inc., 1964), pp. 34–66.

3. Seward Hiltner, *Pastoral Counseling* (Abingdon-Cokesbury Press, 1949).

4. Carroll A. Wise, *Pastoral Counseling: Its Theory and Practice* (Harper & Brothers, 1951).

5. Carl R. Rogers, *Counseling and Psychotherapy* (Houghton Mifflin Company, 1942).

6. Howard J. Clinebell, Jr., *Basic Types of Pastoral Counseling* (Abingdon Press, 1966), p. 28.

7. *Ibid.,* pp. 27–28.

8. Wayne E. Oates, *Protestant Pastoral Counseling* (The Westminster Press, 1962), p. 168.

9. Gerald Caplan, *Principles of Preventive Psychiatry* (Basic Books, Inc., 1964).

10. *Ibid.,* p. 30.

11. *Ibid.,* pp. 16–17.

12. *Ibid.,* pp. 31–34.

13. Granger Westberg, lecture at the Conference on Medicine and Religion, University of California Conference Center at Arrowhead, October, 1966.

14. Glenn E. Whitlock, "Psychotherapy and a Christian Understanding of Man," *Pastoral Psychology,* Vol. XVIII, No. 171 (Feb. 1967).

15. Charlotte Buhler, *Values in Psychotherapy* (The Free Press of Glencoe, Inc., 1962).

16. R. Finley Gayle, Jr., M.D., "Conflict and Cooperation Between

Psychiatry and Religion," Annual Meeting of the American Psychiatric Association, Chicago, April 30, 1956.

17. "Some Considerations of Early Attempts at Cooperation Between Religion and Psychiatry" (Group for the Advancement of Psychiatry, March, 1958).

18. "Why Pastoral Psychology?—An Editorial," *Pastoral Psychology*, Vol. I, No. 1 (Feb., 1950), p. 5.

19. Anton Boisen, quoted by Fred Eastman in, "Father of the Clinical Pastoral Movement," *Journal of Pastoral Care*, Vol. V, No. 1 (Spring, 1951), p. 5.

20. Jeffrey K. Hadden and Raymond C. Rymph, "The Marching Ministers," *Transaction*, Vol. III, No. 6 (Sept.–Oct., 1966), pp. 38–42.

21. James E. Wallace, "A Reforming Church and New Tensions," unpublished manuscript, used by permission. The conceptualization represented by Figure 3 was originally adapted from William M. Evan, "Power, Bargaining and Law: A Preliminary Analysis of Labor Arbitration Cases," *Social Problems*, Vol. 7 (1959), pp. 4–15.

22. Samuel W. Blizzard, "The Parish Minister's Self-image of His Master Role," *Pastoral Psychology*, Vol. IX, No. 89 (Dec., 1958), pp. 25–32; "The Protestant Parish Minister's Integrating Roles," *Religious Education*, Vol. 53, No. 4 (July–Aug., 1958), pp. 374–380; "The Minister's Dilemma," *The Christian Century*, April 25, 1956, pp. 508–509; and Donald P. Smith, *Clergy in the Cross Fire* (The Westminster Press, 1973).

23. Duane Parker, "Pastoral Consultation Through a Community Mental Health Center," *Pastoral Psychology*, Vol. XVII, No. 164 (May, 1966), pp. 42–47.

24. Caplan, *op. cit.*, pp. 214–230.

25. *Ibid.*, p. 214.

26. Glenn E. Whitlock, *From Call to Service: The Making of a Minister* (The Westminster Press, 1968).

27. H. Richard Niebuhr in collaboration with Daniel Day Williams and James M. Gustafson, *The Purpose of the Church and Its Ministry* (Harper & Brothers, 1956), and Daniel Day Williams, *The Care of Souls* (Harper & Brothers, 1951).

28. Caplan, *op. cit.*, p. 217.

29. *Ibid.*, p. 219.

30. Whitlock, *From Call to Service*.

31. Caplan, *op. cit.*, pp. 219–227.

32. *Ibid.*, p. 223.

33. Adapted from Carl A. Whitaker and Thomas P. Malone, *The Roots of Psychotherapy* (McGraw-Hill Book Co., Inc., The Blakiston Division, 1953).

34. Caplan, *op. cit.*, p. 225.

35. *Ibid.*, p. 228.

36. Bruce P. Dohrenwend, "Some Aspects of the Appraisal of Abnormal Behavior by the Leaders in an Urban Area," *American Psychologist*, Vol. 17, No. 4 (April, 1962), p. 197.

37. *Ibid.*

38. Whitlock, *From Call to Service*, pp. 79–83.

39. Niebuhr, *op. cit.*, pp. 79–94.

40. Blizzard, "The Parish Minister's Self-image," pp. 25–32.

41. Quoted in Richard V. McCann, *The Churches and Mental Health*, Joint Commission on Mental Illness and Health, Monograph Series No. 8 (Basic Books, Inc., Publishers, 1962), p. 101.

42. Edward John Carnell, "Fundamentalism," in Marion Halverson and Arthur A. Cohen (eds.), *Handbook of Christian Theology* (Meridian Books, Inc., Living Age Book, 1958), pp. 142–143.

43. Milton Rokeach, *The Open and Closed Mind* (Basic Books, Inc., Publishers, 1960).

44. Daniel Day Williams, *What Present-Day Theologians Are Thinking* (Harper & Brothers, 1952).

45. Gordon MacInnes, "Paper Given to a Group of Presbyterian Ministers," unpublished manuscript. Used by permission.

46. Consultative guidelines for pastoral consultation worked out in collaboration with William J. Sullivan, M.D.

47. Abraham A. Low, *Mental Health Through Will-Training*, 14th ed. (Christopher Publishing House, 1966).

48. Caplan, *op. cit.*, p. 35.

49. *Ibid.*, p. 36.

50. D. C. Klein and E. Lindemann, "Preventive Intervention in Individual and Family Crisis Situations," in Gerald Caplan (ed.), *Prevention of Mental Disorders in Children: Initial Explorations* (Basic Books, Inc., Publishers, 1961), Ch. VII.

51. Caplan, *op. cit.*, pp. 40–41.

52. Glenn E. Whitlock, "Counseling in Crisis Situations," *The Pastoral Counselor*, Vol. V, No. 2 (Winter, 1967), p. 40.

53. Gerald F. Jacobson, lecture, South Bay Mental Health Center, 1967. A more complete treatment appeared in the special issue of *Pastoral Psychology* on Crisis Intervention Counseling, Vol. XXI, No. 203 (April, 1970), pp. 21–28.

54. G. F. Jacobson, D. M. Wilner, W. E. Morley, S. Schneider, M. Strickler, and G. J. Sommer, "The Scope and Practice of an Early-Access Brief Treatment Psychiatric Center," *The American Journal of Psychiatry*, Vol. 121, No. 12 (June, 1965), pp. 1176–1182.

55. Whitlock, "Counseling in Crisis Situations," p. 41. The concept of the two stages is from Gerald Caplan.

56. Gerald F. Jacobson, Martin Strickler, and Wilbur E. Morley, "Generic and Individual Approaches to Crisis Intervention," paper presented before the Mental Health Section of the American Public Health Association at the 94th Annual Meeting in San Francisco. It also appears in *Pastoral Psychology*, Vol. XXI, No. 203 (April, 1970), pp. 17–18.

57. *Ibid.*, p. 7.

58. Whitlock, "Counseling in Crisis Situations," p. 41.

59. Clinebell, *op. cit.*, pp. 139–156.

60. Jacobson, Strickler, and Morley, *loc. cit.*

61. Jacobson, lecture at the South Bay Mental Health Center, 1967.

62. Erich Lindemann, "Symptomatology and Management of Acute Grief," *The American Journal of Psychiatry*, Vol. 101, No. 2 (Sept., 1944).

63. Louis I. Dublin, quoted by Earl A. Grollman in "Rabbinical Counseling and Suicide" in *Rabbinical Counseling*, ed. by Earl A. Grollman (Bloch Publishing Company, Inc., 1966), p. 130.

64. *Ibid.*, p. 129.

65. Norman L. Farberow and Edwin S. Shneidman (eds.), *The Cry for Help* (McGraw-Hill Book Co., Inc., The Blakiston Division, 1961). See also Edwin S. Shneidman, Norman L. Farberow, and Robert E. Litman, *The Psychology of Suicide* (Science House, Inc., 1970), and Earl Grollman, *Suicide* (Beacon Press, Inc., 1971).

66. Emile Durkheim, *Suicide*, tr. by John A. Spaulding and George Simpson (Free Press, 1951).

67. Edwin S. Shneidman, "Classifications of Suicidal Phenomena," *Bulletin of Suicidology* (National Institute of Mental Health, Government Printing Office, July, 1968), p. 2.

68. *Ibid.*, p. 4.

69. *Ibid.*, pp. 5–6.

70. *Ibid.*, pp. 6–7.

71. *Ibid.*, pp. 7–8.

72. Paul Pretzel, lecture at South Bay Mental Health Center, 1967. An elaboration of his views has appeared in "The Role of the Clergyman in Suicide Prevention," in *Pastoral Psychology*, Vol. XXI, No. 203 (April, 1970), and most recently in *Understanding and Counseling the Suicidal Person* (Abingdon Press, 1972).

73. M. Brewster Smith, "The Revolution in Mental-Health Care —A 'Bold New Approach'?" in *Transaction*, April, 1968, p. 19.

74. Richard W. Thoreson, Charles J. Kranskopf, Charles A. McAleer, and H. David Wenger, "The Future for Applied Psychology," *American Psychologist*, Vol. 27, No. 2 (Feb., 1972), p. 136.

Bibliography

TOPICAL

A. *Preventive or Community Psychology*

Action for Mental Health, Report of the Joint Commission on Mental Illness and Health. Basic Books, Inc., Publishers, 1961.

Caplan, Gerald (ed.), *Prevention of Mental Disorders in Children: Initial Explorations.* Basic Books, Inc., Publishers, 1961.

———— *Principles of Preventive Psychiatry.* Basic Books, Inc., Publishers, 1964.

———— *The Theory and Practice of Mental Health Consultation.* Basic Books, Inc., Publishers, 1970.

Cook, Patrick E. (ed.), *Community Psychology and Community Mental Health: Introductory Readings.* Holden-Day, Inc., 1970.

Dumont, Matthew P., M.D., *The Absurd Healer: Perspectives of a Community Psychiatrist.* Science House, Inc., 1968.

Rosenblum, G. (ed.), *Issues in Community Psychology and Preventive Mental Health* (The Task Force on Community Mental Health, Division 27 of APA). Behavioral Publications, 1971.

B. *Crisis Intervention Theory and Practice*

Aguilera, Donna C., Messick, Janice M., and Farrell, Mariene S., *Crisis Intervention: Theory and Methodology.* The C. V. Mosby Company, Publishers, 1970.

Langsley, Donald G., and Kaplan, David, *The Treatment of Families in Crisis.* Grune & Stratton, Inc., 1968.

Parad, Howard J. (ed.), *Crisis Intervention: Selected Readings.* Family Service Association of America, 1965.

Whitlock, Glenn E. (Guest Ed.), Special Issue on "Crisis Intervention Counseling," *Pastoral Psychology,* Vol. XXI, No. 203 (April, 1970).

C. *Suicide Prevention and Treatment*

Farber, Maurice L., *Theory of Suicide.* Funk & Wagnalls Company, Inc., 1969.

Farberow, Norman L., and Shneidman, Edwin S. (eds.), *The Cry for Help.* McGraw-Hill Book Co., Inc., 1961.

Grollman, Earl, *Suicide.* Beacon Press, Inc., 1971.

Meerloo, Joost A. M., *Suicide and Mass Suicide.* E. P. Dutton & Co., 1968.

Pretzel, Paul W., *Understanding and Counseling the Suicidal Person.* Abingdon Press, 1972.

Shneidman, Edwin S., and Farberow, Norman L., *Clues to Suicide.* McGraw-Hill Book Co., Inc., 1957.

Shneidman, Edwin S., Farberow, Norman L., and Litman, Robert E., *The Psychology of Suicide.* Science House, Inc., 1970.

D. *The Church or Temple and Mental Health*

Clebsch, William A., and Jaekle, Charles R., *Pastoral Care in Historical Perspective*. Prentice-Hall, Inc., 1964.

Clinebell, Howard J., Jr., *Basic Types of Pastoral Counseling*. Abingdon Press, 1966.

———— (ed.), *Community Mental Health: The Role of Church and Temple*. Abingdon Press, 1970.

Grollman, Earl A. (ed.), *Rabbinical Counseling*. Bloch Publishing Company, Inc., 1966.

———— *Pastoral Counseling*. Abingdon Press, 1949.

Hiltner, Seward, *Preface to Pastoral Theology*. Abingdon Press, 1958.

McCann, Richard V., *The Churches and Mental Health* (Joint Commission on Mental Illness and Health, Monograph Series No. 8). Basic Books, Inc., Publishers, 1962.

Niebuhr, H. Richard, in collaboration with Williams, Daniel Day, and Gustafson, James M., *The Purpose of the Church and Its Ministry*. Harper & Brothers, 1956.

Oates, Wayne E., *Protestant Pastoral Counseling*. The Westminster Press, 1962.

Westberg, Granger E., and Draper, Edgar, M.D., *Community Psychiatry and the Clergyman*. Charles C Thomas, Publisher, 1966.

Whitlock, Glenn E., *From Call to Service: The Making of a Minister*. The Westminster Press, 1968.

Williams, Daniel Day, *The Care of Souls*. Harper & Brothers, 1951.

Wise, Carroll A., *Pastoral Counseling: Its Theory and Practice*. Harper & Brothers, 1951.

Selected Journals

Community Mental Health Journal, Behavioral Publications, Inc., 2852 Broadway, New York, N.Y. 10025.

Crisis and Change, Quarterly, Harvard Medical School Psychiatry Department, Laboratory of Community Psychiatry, 58 Fenwood Road, Boston, Mass. 02115.

Journal of Pastoral Care, Association for Clinical Pastoral Education, Inc., Suite 450, 475 Riverside Drive, New York, N.Y. 10027.

Life Threatening Behavior, American Association of Suicidology, Behavioral Publications, Inc., 2852 Broadway, New York, N.Y. 10025.

Pastoral Psychology, 400 Community Drive, Manhasset, N.Y. 11030.